global obscenities

global obscenities

patriarchy,

capitalism,

and the lure of

cyberfantasy

zillah eisenstein

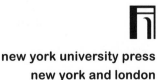

new york university press
new york and london

new york university press
New York and London

© 1998 by New York University
All rights reserved

Library of Congress Cataloging-in-Publication Data
Eisenstein, Zillah R.
Global obscenities : patriarchy, capitalism, and the lure of
cyberfantasy / Zillah Eisenstein.
p.   cm.
Includes index.
ISBN 0-8147-2205-9 (hardcover : alk. paper). — ISBN 0-8147-2206-7
(pbk. : alk. paper)
1. Feminist theory. 2. Marxian economics. 3. Cyberspace.
I. Title.
HQ1190.E38   1998
305.42'01—dc21   98-25275
                            CIP

New York University Press books are printed on acid-free paper,
and their binding materials are chosen for strength and durability.

Manufactured in the United States of America

10 9 8 7 6 5 4 3 2 1

For my beloved mother, Fannie Price Eisenstein

contents

acknowledgments

My writing is a process that necessitates the recognition of many others. My faithful readers and critics allow me to rethink and rework ideas in dialogue with them. Without them, I would not be able to write as I do. Miriam Brody, Rosalind Petchesky, and Patricia Zimmermann each read and commented on the full manuscript in its entirety and Miriam actually read it a second time. I have come to depend on their intellectual rigor immensely, and I deeply appreciate their continuous support. My thanks also to Frank Wood, Chandra Mohanty, Susan Buck-Morss, Anna-Marie Smith, Thomas Shevory, and Asma Barlas for reading several chapters in early draft form.

Sylvestre Marlaud, my research assistant, was invaluable in finding obscure materials, both in hard copy and on the net. Jim Meyer greatly assisted me in finding the latest books on cyberspace. Jill Swenson was very helpful in suggesting media-related sources. Frank Wood of the Cornell Theory Center took me on several excursions into virtual reality.

Donna Freedline helped me sort through my enormous correspondence related to this book project. Sarah Dean assisted me with the final copy.

My daughter Sarah insisted that she was better equipped to search and explore cyberspace than I was. I thank her for my early excursions to places unknown.

My students at Ithaca College have played a significant role in this book. In two seminars, Gender in Cyberspace (fall 1996) and Debates in Feminism (fall 1997), students researched the net for its cybersexual, cybergender, and cyberfeminist aspects. Special thanks to Leigh Ann Kuiken, Katy Pennypacker, Eliza Minsch, and Laura Williams.

I must also thank those in my life who sustain me and make it possible for me to work as I do. In this increasingly privatized world I feel lucky to have such a rich network of people to depend on. Deep thanks to Fannie Price Eisenstein, Ellen Wade, Rebecca Riley, Carla Golden, Mary Katzenstein, Mary Ryan, Julia Price Eisenstein, Sarah Eisenstein Stumbar, bell hooks, Richard Stumbar, Patty Zimmermann, Chandra Mohanty, Toni House, Isaac Kramnick, Rosalind Petchesky, Linda Zerilli, Susan Buck-Morss, Bernie Wohl, and Miriam Brody.

Lastly, I wish to thank Cecelia Cancellaro for suggesting that I consider working with Niko Pfund at New York University Press. And I wish to thank Niko for being such a supportive and spectacular editor. Thanks also to the incredible staff at NYU Press for their expeditious work and varied talents used in the last stages of producing the book: Despina Papazoglou Gimbel, Andrew Katz, Nicole Sanfilippo, David Updike, and Stewart Cauley. Of course, I alone am responsible for any shortcomings of this book.

I cannot conclude my acknowledgments without mentioning my younger sister, Giah Eisenstein. I started writing this book shortly before she was diagnosed with ovarian cancer. As she bravely and desperately fought for her life—over and over again—I was painfully reminded of the limits of REAL bodies. I am sure that her death provoked some of the despair written into this book. But I am also as sure that her incredible tenacity against enormous odds is also written into my sense of possibility.

introduction

Some 800 million people are starving across the globe. Women and girls represent approximately 60 percent of the billion or so people earning one dollar a day or less. However, in countries labeled democratic, a new kind of excessive wealth exists in which billionaires are allowed to amass as much as they can with few limits. New levels of arrogance emerge just as the nation-state is being overshadowed by transnational corporations.

Meanwhile, corporations displace countries. Of the world's largest one hundred economies, fifty-one are corporations, not countries. The two hundred largest corporations hire less than three-fourths of one percent of the world's work force but account for 28 percent of the global market. The five hundred biggest corporations account for 70 percent of world trade. No surprise that Amnesty International now reports on corporations as well as nation-states.[1]

Class exploitation seems to be back with a vengeance, and women and girls—especially those in third-world-south countries—appear to take the brunt of it. But this racializing of gender also applies in first-world-north countries. The new geographies of power are located and layered across the first/third-world divide. In order to understand this POWER we must theorize its patriarchal and racialized moorings.

This book sets out to theorize the web of globalized consumer capital and its racialized/sexualized underbelly. It explores the tensions between 'really' real, fantasy real, and virtually real in our highly media-ted world. I pluralize 'the' real—unmediated reality that is never quite knowable as such, media-ted viewings that are always in play, and cyberconstructions of knowing—while also demanding a reading of the power relations defining these relations.

These layerings of power, which are constructed, articulated, and distributed by the cyber-media complex of transnational capital, form a complicated web. I seek to delineate the webbed and layered relations of global power. Each chapter prioritizes one layering within the web while also articulating the intricate local and transnational marbled whole. The transnational systems of power I interrogate are clearly defined, but also interlinked. Therefore the chapters are also webbed, multilayered, and overlapping.

The web of transnational capital is not seamless and open, with no center. Rather, the power of capital's cyber-media complex is hierarchical, grossly unequal, AND dispersed. I show how cybertechnologies rearticulate systems of power AND undo them. The centers of power are always shifting, which is different from saying that power has no specific location.

As spaces for public life are downsized and emptied of their interactive and deliberative purposes, people live in more isolating and privatized conditions. In first-world-north countries, those who can afford to often seek refuge in private schools, private housing enclaves, private gyms, private playgrounds, and private transportation. Computer technologies assist these processes AND can provide ways of escape for those fortunate to have access.

The demise of government's public regard for its poor is not one and the same with the demise of the nation-state. Rather, the nation-state is being restructured by the needs of transnational capital while commitments to social responsibility are being trampled. Because of the transitional nature of geographical and economic nations, I do not capitalize the names of countries in my writing. However, I retain capitalization of cities because of their renewed transnational commercial status in the twenty-first century.

Almost twenty years ago I edited the book *Capitalist Patriarchy and the Case for Socialist Feminism*.[2] That book began a dialogue between Karl Marx's theory of exploitation and radical feminism's recognition of women as a sexual class. My writing and politics since then have demanded a series of reworkings of Marx's undertheorized recognition of patriarchal and racialized oppression. Thus, I seek to explicate the racial and gendered structurings of power: the processes by which biological bodies, sexed and colored, are simultaneously encoded with artificial/political meaning.[3]

I now return to Marx's theory of exploitation, but in a new fashion. I use it to expose the distinct power relations of racialized patriarchy and their unique representation/exploitation in cyber-media-capitalist culture. I then thread this inside the complicated exchanges of women's and girls' labor around the world.

So, Marx and Engels had it partially right and partially wrong in the *Communist Manifesto*.[4] There are new ways to think through to their call for unified action from the workers of the world. Today, their declaration should read: WOMEN/ GIRLS OF THE WORLD—ACROSS YOUR DIFFERENCES— UNITE!

This may seem like an unreal political position for today. But today's reality is also unreal, and fantasy, and virtual. Let me see if I can convince you.

1
seeing

Virtual Globes and Cyberpublics

seeing

I want to talk about creating democracy—for people, especially women and girls—across the globe. In this democracy, no one would be left hungry or without a job. No one could be forced to birth a child. No one would remain illiterate. No one would have to breathe contaminated air. It would be a democracy that recognized the unique individual differences of each person while allowing that person the access needed to develop her or his potential for a creative and sustainable life.

This means I must reclaim the public realm—as an imagined IDEA that presumes the interconnectedness of people and their responsibility for each other. This is a hard sell, particularly since the fall of communist statism and the destruction of the social welfare states of the west. But my notion of 'public' is not one and the same with activist government, or corporate interests, or civil society.

Rather, my 'public' is socially constructed—part real, part imagined—and requires a politics beyond selfish individualism, governmental privatization, and state corruption. It creatively invokes an imagined space defined by individuals' freedom alongside their social responsibility. It is where the varied demands for equality are negotiated. It is where the relational aspects of individual needs are uncovered. The IDEA of 'public' allows that individual needs are met socially and collectively, and collective needs are identified individually.

My notion of 'public' then is both a process—of thinking through and beyond the self—AND a place where this happens. It is both verb AND noun, an attitude AND a location, an imagined space AND also real.[1]

Have I lost you before I have begun? Some of you will not agree with my notion of publicness. Some, though sympathetic, will say I am living in a fantasy land, that I might as well move to Oz and click my red ruby slippers.[2] But who's to say? I have a thirteen-year-old daughter and I want her to live in a different world. I am tired of the reigning political chatter: that government must do less, people must do more for themselves, that the united states is thriving economically and presents the only viable alternative for third- and fourth-world countries of the south to emulate. Instead, new publics and new ways of governing must be imagined and created.

There is no easy way to enter my discussion. I therefore ask you to travel with me on a somewhat bumpy and seemingly disconnected journey.

Marshall McLuhan notwithstanding, the globe is not a village. While some sign on to the internet to chat, others still haul water and firewood daily. Some are unknowingly infected with AIDS while others can afford state-of-the-art medications to combat it.

Governments scale down and privatize more and more services and create new communities in need. Meanwhile, the very notion of taking responsibility or caring for 'the' public health, or public education, or public housing loses credibility in the minds of the very officials who were once supposed to articulate such a commitment.

The process of NOT seeing and hoping has become essential in the creation of a privatized globe. And yet, media's telecommunications networks and cyberspaces connect and create other imaginings and fantasies that both initiate democratic visions and completely undermine them.

So, who is looking at what? And how is the 'reel' seen? What is real in this new mix of media-ted experiences? How does one construct this nonmaterialist materialism to understand imaginaries, fantasy, and virtuality—simulations of 'the' real? I here examine the realm of virtuality, the screen, the re-presentation of the globe through Disney's eyes, in order to return eventually—and differently—to the REAL of hauling water. The real is pluralized today through digital and cyber-mediated appearances. And the realm of appearance seems real and becomes real while genuine systems of power are submerged from view.

Searching for Democracy in New Publics

The tension between privacy and publicness has long structured the bourgeois notion of democratic living. This structure is not without its problems. It has been a foundation of the racist/masculinist privileging of citizenship. The increased privatization of western societies and the de-publicizing of government responsibility has reconfigured the dynamic of racial/patriarchal privilege. Patriarchal societies look different as more women of color work in public spaces, although the risks these women face often remain the same. The selfishness of privatization reframes the privileging of white men for the twenty-first century. Meanwhile, it is hard to sort fact from fiction, real from virtual, hyperreal from everyday life.

"Think globally, act locally," the saying goes. But it is too difficult to do either as public space declines and is taken over by 'the' private. Giddy endorsements of Barnes and Noble and Niketown as townsquares aside, the public has declined as a space/idea where people meet, share with others, and come to care about each other. Think of the dismal state of the public schools in most big cities today. Simultaneously, governments in advanced capitalist nations have shifted their rhetoric from encouraging a responsibility for public life to trumpeting the private sector of volunteerism.

Privatized individualism and volunteerism mask a dependency on patriarchal and racialized forms of familialism. And this mask covers the labor of women of all colors, as well as multiple realities of networked support that are already stretched as far as they can go. As government programs are downsized or relegated to the privatized economy, the needs that they no longer meet are relocated to a fantasized family life that certainly does not exist now and probably never did.

As advanced capitalism—or global capital in its racialized and sexualized guises—proceeds to destroy public arenas of support for democracy, power is quietly siphoned out of the once social service/public spaces of nation-states. This hollowed-out AND revamped government apparatus is positioned impotently against global capital. As the global economy and its media/medium of the culture industry become more and more autonomous from national governments it may matter less and less who occupies these traditional seats of power, now increasingly virtual. The u.s. government is not 'really' powerful in its relationship to transnational media/corporate interests although it retains a crushing power over the poor. Though never autonomous from capital, nation-states have never been as dependent on it as they are at present.

Maybe this is in part why mainstream politics appears so vacuous and emptied of consequence. Bob Dole seemed out of touch and beside the point in the 1996 presidential election. Bill Clinton seems like such a waffler, as he says so much but delivers so little. The women elected to public office today may be too late to do any good.[3] David Dinkins wondered the same thing about his mayoral election in New York City.

The 'real' of power is open to negotiation. As consumer culture facilitates profit-making alongside a symbolic discourse of decadent individual freedom, the media of these messages weave a symbolic order that is not simply true or false, virtual or real. Murphy Brown, a t.v. character, was criticized by former vice-president Dan Quayle as though she were a 'real' single mother; O. J. Simpson became something other than the defendant in a murder trial; the Gulf War was won, and 'not' really won; Princess Diana in death became a great humanitarian who challenged the british monarchy.

In this process of depicting, representing, and symbolizing the 'real' the multimedia of knowing—t.v., internet, print media—have become more and more insidious as they construct new locations that disperse power. Media such as t.v. talk shows, news programs, tabloids, and cyberspace chat rooms undermine the divide between public and private discourse. If privacy is public-ized, publicness is privatized and neither remains as it was—both are lost. If everything is known, there is nothing left to know.

So we know our president's secrets: he has had multiple affairs, an abusive and alcoholic father, little discipline, and so on. We know this, but we really know nothing at all. They are no longer secrets, but they are not 'real' information that matters, either. It is also information I need to forget as I pretend that he is a president with power to affect things. But I do remember enough of these secrets to know that little is what it seems. Then, I am expected to pretend anyway.

Politics, although always in part theater, raises this process of symbolizing the 'real' to new heights. The Republican Revolution of 1994 clearly was not what it seemed. At first it SEEMED that the voting public was asking for sweeping change and an end to government as we have known it. But by 1996 Newt Gingrich was in disfavor. He just SEEMED too brutish and mean. But who knows how long this ever lasts, or if it does not, why it does not. Who 'really' believes this matters?

However, it does really matter to some. It matters particularly for those who have lost their safety net, or who cannot get a green card. But political routes have shifted toward transnational capital and its telecommunications networks. C. W. Mills might say that the military-industrial-cultural complex locates 'real' power at multiple and interconnected sites. The sites shift as the global telecommunications complex becomes more sophisticated and concentrated. I call this concentrated core of dispersed power a cyber-media complex of corporatist capital.[4] And this complex operates to renegotiate the global systems of patriarchal and racialized hierarchy.

It is hard to see the sites of power as they shift and fluctuate today. The military has been shrinking since 1989, yet it remains a major source of u.s. global power. Deindustrialization is transforming first-world economies. And consumer culture media-ted through tele/cyber communications dominates everything else. The sites of power are singular and plural. If the cultural logic of capitalism is "to produce a uniform culture of pure consumption."[5] then the locations of power, though more dispersed inside and outside the nation, are also more concentrated in the transnational cyber-media corporate complex.

Seeing is key. And we see through media-ted forms that can make knowing almost impossible. Imaginaries—of the globe and cyberspace—attempt to displace and reconfigure the excessive greed and wealth of transnational capital. We need a revamped materialism that will allow us to see the virtual realities of the globe. I want a class-conscious, race-conscious, feminist critique of the 'virtual' realm of cyberspace and media-ted telecommunications. Then, maybe we can reconfigure a viewing of a public with 'real' possibilities for democracy.

On Virtual Marxism

The extremes of wealth and poverty within the united states also mirror the extremes across the globe. The wealthiest 20 percent of u.s. citizens received 99 percent of the total gain in marketable wealth between 1983 and 1989. More than 38 million people live in poverty in the united states, of whom more than 40 percent are under eighteen years of age.[6] In his last major address as labor secretary, Robert Reich made it clear that the broadly shared prosperity of the post–World War II era is gone.[7] Meanwhile, the joblessness and poverty among Black americans becomes more entrenched as "work disappears."[8]

Economic inequality blooms alongside cyber freedom. Technological empowerment has no trickle-down effect for the poor.[9] Although Bill Clinton and Al Gore talk about hooking up every child to the internet, it is ludicrous to speak of access to the information highway in a country, and a world, defined by economic and societal inequality. But government is not on the side of the poor. The u.s. government recently handed over almost $100 billion worth of free space on the airwaves to enhance u.s. corporate telecommunications power globally.[10]

Advanced capitalism must be confronted by a critique that locates excessive profits as a key problem for first-world-north and third-world-south countries alike. The new extremes of opulent wealth and horrific poverty found in any city across the globe are supported by a transnational sexual division of labor that increasingly demands extraordinary amounts of labor from women. As nations across the globe are privatized and the public-regarding spirit of governmental responsibility recedes, the new burdens of this individualism fall especially upon women and girls.

But if this is 'the' real, it is not what we see through the mediated discourses of racialized patriarchy via global capital. Instead, the visual images that are mediated for us through CNN, MTV, the internet, and so on displace and remove the relations of power and naturalize what we see, making it appear ordinary and inevitable.

Jean Baudrillard believes that the virtual—as the symbolic rather than the actual—becomes a substitute for depiction. Information "obliterates the original reference" to capital, technology, and power.[11] Technologies and their forms of communication define the parameters of everyday life today with a relative "autonomization" from transnational corporate power.[12]

Commodities become social signifiers. There is no longer a real economy and an unreal advertising world, but rather a "hyperreality, a world of self-referential signs."[13] In hyperreal-

ity, a reality without origin, the signifier becomes its own referent.[14] The real is unreal, the unreal real. Advertising and consumption are ruled by the value of the sign, which has a self-re-
ferring hyperreality.[15]

Simulacra, copies that no longer have originals, become the
real. "A world of surface" dominates.[16] These self-referential
signs, these simulations, are not fictions that seek to replace the
real. Rather, they are a process of "absorbing the real within itself."[17] Truth is not concealed here because there is no longer
any origin. It is the generation of a real without reality. Simulation then "threatens the difference between 'true' and 'false,'
between 'real' and 'imaginary.'"[18]

The threat is profound, and sometimes Baudrillard collapses
it into complete victory. He says: "It is reality itself today that is
hyperrealist." Digital simulation absorbs the world and wins
out over reality. Reality is reduced into hyperrealism. Information does not matter here because the simulation goes forward.
Our politicians are crooks, but lots of people still vote for them.
The justice system is racist, but it keeps performing its duties
anyhow. Welfare mothers are predominantly white, but people
see them as black. Baudrillard would no doubt call this the
"hallucination of truth."[19]

The "work-real, the production-real, has disappeared" with
the industrial age.[20] In this age of the sign, simulation reigns.
It is hard to know whether one sees signs as pointing to reality,
trying to hide reality, or hiding the absence of the real.[21]

The illusion of reality substitutes for reality. Virtual arenas of
electronic cyberspace accentuate this substitution. Simulation
and real blur information. The virtual, deployed abstractly, has
overtaken the actual.[22] The signifieds and signifiers of politics
become what politics is. Moments of origin are emptied of their
meaning. Of course, illusion masquerading as truth is hardly a

new phenomenon. However, these processes are accentuated by the new possibilities of cyber-media technologies.

For Baudrillard, the codes we listen to no longer refer back to any subjective or objective 'reality.' The signifier becomes its own referent, and the "sign no longer designates anything at all."[23] Signs simply refer back to other signs. Paul Patton calls this hyperrealist logic: the distinction between virtual and actual no longer holds while the virtual deters the real.[24]

Signs come to have a life of their own. One can see 'Blackness' where it does not exist—for instance, a Puerto Rican seeming or acting 'Black.' One can see gender where only sex exists—a female acting or seeming like a man. But the 'reality' of racism and sexism is what allows these signs their meaning, which is already in place. It is not ALL simulacra. Power and oppression are not simply signs with no origin.

Baudrillard is consumed by the reality of illusions and phantasms. For him, Disneyland presents an imaginary in order to make everything else seem real. The issue is no longer the false representation of reality but "of concealing the fact that the real is no longer real, and thus of saving the reality principle." The Disneyland imaginary becomes a "deterrence machine" that "rejuvenate[s] in reverse the fiction of the real."[25]

Maybe this is why theme parks are so popular today. Surrogate experience and synthetic settings stand in for 'real' life. What we get is a "real fake" like the hotel/casino New York, New York, in Las Vegas. One can pretend to be in New York without experiencing all the problems of the subways. Defects and problems are removed. New York becomes user-friendly.[26] Virtuality has no predefined limits. Cyberspace, as one location of the virtual, makes the "artificial as realistic as, and even more realistic than, the real."[27]

The virtual is real and the real is also virtual. Each is, in part, a construction of the other. Signs signify and they also float freely. Virtual worlds do not exist merely in technology, nor purely in the mind of the user, but "between internal mental constructs and technologically generated representations of these constructs." There is an illusion of reality because individuals treat "imaginings as if they were real."[28]

It is significant that in so many arenas of life we are asked to dichotomize, to choose between the real and the ideal. The fluidity between these realms is thus denied. When Marx critiques Hegel for his nonmaterialism, we are left with Marx's overly materialist definition of ideology. When Baudrillard critiques Marx for overstating the materialist analysis of production, which is devoid of "language, signs and communication in general," he excessively privileges the "whole murky field of signification and communication."[29]

Yet, I agree with Baudrillard that the very "production of meaning, messages and signs poses a crucial problem to revolutionary theory," and that in some sense Marxist theory is not helpful here. It cannot sufficiently explain the process by which the hyperreal operates as its own logic. The process of production is often separated from its sign.[30] Therefore, it is not enough to say that the mass media are a mere tool of ideological manipulation, but neither are they simply conveying messages. There is a relatively autonomous logic to the signification of capital, which is not wholly grasped by a mirror image of production.[31] For Baudrillard, 'the' commodity is just one form of signification, *and* these other signs have no referent. "Capitalism detaches the signifier from the signified, making the signifier its own signified."[32]

For example, in the past money represented some material and useful thing. It was merely a token to facilitate complex barter. Then money became detached from the thing and an object of desire in itself. The signifier is detached from the signified. Now things are even more detached—the signifier of the commodity becomes the valued thing, and a pair of NIKE shoes is worth more than the kid wearing them.

The Gulf War was both signifier and sign. But for Baudrillard "the mode of signification" is one and the same with the "monopoly of the code." The sign becomes its own "super-ideology," sort of like the hyperreal.[33] All becomes fiction, and there is no real.

This is not quite right in my mind because the Gulf War *did* 'happen.' And Nicole Brown *was* murdered. And Princess Di *is* more fantasy than she is of 'of the people.' And right-wing militants *do* blow up buildings. Yet, Baudrillard is right when he says that the war was a sham, that we did not view 'the' war, that there was a captive t.v. audience, and that what they saw on-screen was fabricated. But, there was *also* the 'fact' that over 200,000 people died in this fabricated war.[34]

The war was both illusory and horrifically real. The tricky part of the virtual/real, hyper/simple, and t.v./everyday life dichotomies is that they partially collapse into each other. Each/both are powerfully symbolic. Each played a part in constructing the O. J. Simpson 'official' story.[35] Each played a part in constructing Princess Di as a 'real person's princess: a bourgeois, media-savvy aristocrat. In the end it is almost impossible to tease apart fact from fiction because they are simply neither: they are instead two kinds of reality.

Baudrillard comes close to explaining the art of the spectacle today, but he also overstates it. Whether it is bosnia, or rwanda, or Rodney King, or welfare mothers, or 'the' government, each is a sign *and* also real.

Baudrillard tells us that the simulators of war have won and that when there is a 'real' war no one will be able to tell the difference.[36] I doubt iraqi women would concur. They can tell the difference between real and unreal by the black air they breathe and the blackened corpses that once were their loved ones.

Yet, Baudrillard is right when he describes the Gulf War as a post-cold-war strategy of "monopolistic deterrence."[37] The part of the war that was electronic/hyperreal did neutralize and consensualize the war, domestically, for a short piece of time. In large part this was orchestrated by the pentagon via CNN. Television news did not just distribute information, it constituted the information—and it did so dangerously, by fabricating non-communication as dialogue. T.V. screens isolated the war by presenting it, according to Baudrillard, "as speech without response."[38]

Media-ted information privileges passive reception rather than active reciprocity. Call-in talk shows *mimic* dialogue more than they encourage liberatory exchange.[39] The new technologies of communication—e-mail, faxes, teleconferencing—hold out autonomized spheres of democratic possibility, but these exist alongside and within established antidemocratic parameters. The democratic possibilities of virtual media interlace with the reality that people of color, white women, and girls across the globe have less access to a living wage, reproductive health care, computers, and phone lines.

When we speak of information highways, we need to remember that one out of three women worldwide is illiterate and spends a significant portion of her day performing essentials like collecting wood and drawing water. On the other hand, cyberspace requires a phone line, and only one in five people across the globe have them.[40] In the united states, nearly one in five Black and Hispanic households do not have phone lines; among poor women heading households with small children, close to half do not.[41]

One must make enormous leaps back and forth to connect the different extremes and realities that constitute the challenges of a liberatory democracy for tomorrow.

Privatization and Its New Shifting Publics

The concept of "public" shifts around and invariably has multiple meanings. The public arena has long been identified by feminists for its maleness and its masculinist authority. The public has *also* been subsumed as one and the same with government, or the economy. Other times it is viewed as anything that is not private, or tied to family life.[42] For Jürgen Habermas the ideal public is the area of discussion and exchange.[43] For Walter Lippmann it is the phantom notion of a shared consensus.[44] Since the revolutions of 1989 western, news correspondents depict it as a suspect arena that tramples on individual freedoms. Neoliberals link the public realm with the inadequacies of government.

Yet, when Bill Clinton was elected president in 1992, many voted for him because they thought he would devise a notion of public health to meet the crises of private health care. In a 1995 *New York Times*/CBS News Poll almost two-thirds of those interviewed said they believed government should take care of those people who cannot take care of themselves.[45] Clearly, many still want an active government that assists people and maintains the larger sense of community: clean air, safety controls on products, medical research, food stamps for those in need, and so on. In this view, government has a responsibility to maintain the structural requisites for the public good. This public sphere is where the needs of individuals merge with those of the collective whole: roads, education, drinking water, social discourse, interactivity, and so on.

Governments need to be revised and rebuilt to initiate and sustain networks that allow individuals to inhabit collective spaces. In this sense, a governing body must nurture a sense of collectivity and social responsibility that individuals share. This notion of public recognizes the webbed and intersectional connections between people. It pluralizes an individual's needs beyond the self to others. Someone else's hunger becomes *my* problem, and I improve myself as I address this need. This does not simply mean donating food for the poor, or working at a soup kitchen. Rather, it requires a demand to restructure the economy and its racial/gender hierarchy so that there are no poor.

My thinking about public life—the space where the IDEA of publicness is also lived and nurtured—is not positioned against private life, but neither does it conflate the two arenas. Public and private are not homogeneous categories to begin with. There are several publics, and there are multiple sites for private life. And there are sites where the two intersect: coffee shops, settlement houses, t.v. talk shows, beauty parlors, bars, day care centers.[46]

We must move beyond a simple spatial or literal notion of public/private. Susan Williams asks us to think of the public not as a realm, but as an orientation. We need to contrast the IDEA of publicness, not with privacy, but with selfishness, irresponsibility, and nondemocracy.[47] Publicness becomes a commitment to a collectivity that is never limited to the self, although it does not deny the parameters of individual autonomy.

My notion of public is not a cramped locale between the governmental and the private realm. Rather, it is the 'intersecting relationships' that reconfigure these realms. Publicness assumes a set of responsibilities that recognize the shared and relational meaning of individual experience. This imagined public requires individual freedom alongside available means to actualize choices. One freely chooses AND one really gets what one needs. This arena is not without conflict and tension as differing needs are sorted out. But there is also recognition and celebration of real diversity.

I am reclaiming the IDEA of public and publicness for a radically progressive democracy. 'Public' is imagined, meaning that one must conceptualize beyond the privatized neoliberal politics of the day. There is a big difference between the political imagination I am requesting and the media IMAGINARIES that support and sustain privatized culture. We must dare to imagine a publicness that challenges the excesses of global capital and its racialized and patriarchal structures.

My notion of publicness does not simply augur an activist government because there are too few skeletal remains of such government from which to build. Nor is it simply an imagined arena, just a space of shared interconnected community. It is parts of each: a nonpaternalist, nonauthoritarian, collective and individualist idea of shared access that directly challenges the cyber-media complex of global capital.

The crisis in our sense of publicness is exacerbated by the greed of global corporations. A majority of the world's population is excluded from the new modes of access, and there are signs that more and more people are becoming critical of this situation. In the united states, 44 percent of those interviewed in a 1995 *New York Times* poll about the downsizing of corporations blamed corporations, 44 percent blamed the government, and 60 percent blamed the economic system.[48] But alternatives seem few and far between amid the triumph of capital.[49] Socialism supposedly cared too much about the public and not enough about the individual. Yet, capitalism without a formidable nation-state to set limits is obsessively self-interested.

Philanthropist George Soros worries that excessive individualism can destroy democracy just like excessive statism, or fascism, or communism.[50] As transnational corporations outgrow the 'geographical' nation they become less interested in what happens to the countries they were once located within.[51] Corporations can thus disregard the public good with less consequence to themselves.

The nation-state, though always partly dependent on class formations, becomes more so with the instantaneous transmission of information around the globe. These new forms of communication bypass old borders. Significant sites of globalization are then located in electronic spaces that escape all conventional jurisdiction, as well as borders. Saskia Sassen calls these spaces a realm of new "non-governance."[52]

These same instantaneous transmissions also create a global gaze that can be used to demand that certain standards of democracy be met. For example, public debate has scrutinized Disney's use of offshore sweatshops and starvation wages for its young women/girl workers in haiti, indonesia, and china. Union organizers at the National Labor Coalition have been instrumental in demanding that Disney obey u.s. national standards when hiring workers overseas.[53]

Habermas wonders whether a sense of public can be reconstituted given the present forms of capitalism and its cultural artifacts. The public sphere, he believes, has been dumped by late capitalism; public life eventually withers and is "refeudalized."[54] Global capitalism's attack on nation-state capitalism, Benjamin Barber argues, heralds the demise of democracy.[55] Michael Sandel fears that the onslaught of big capital and its assault on big government has eroded democracy.[56] Small government does not have enough of a civic voice.[57]

The bourgeois nation-state developed with the language and discourse of (liberal) democracy. This construct articulates the public/private divide, which embraces the conundrum of individual and collective existence. We are living through the transition from the bourgeois nation-state to an unknown governance structure of transnational global capital: a nation-state defined by global capital and its racialized, patriarchal, cyber-media-ted relations. This new construct demands a very much downsized and privatized version of social welfare government. It also premises a privatized version of citizenship that replaces public responsibility with individual initiative. Liberal democratic discourse is displaced by neoconservatism, also termed neoliberalism.

The first-world nation-state of the twenty-first century redefines public arenas AS private: less and less is done by governments for individuals, and more is done to ensure corporate competitiveness globally. Private lives even become the metaphor for politics itself. Bob Dole is reduced to his personal struggle with war wounds; Al Gore reduces himself to his sister's suffering from cancer and his son's brush with death; Bill Clinton becomes one and the same with his brother's fight against drug addiction.[58] On the one hand, we are only individuals; on the other hand, we are the globe. The dismantling of the construct of public—the intersection of individuals in communities—is insidious and remarkably effective.

In the war between public and private worlds, privacy is winning for those who are able to claim it. The u.s. culture is becoming "starved for public experiences." Because people are a social species, the more they live without a sense of publicness, the more they seek to find it. Today, "stores entice us into their versions of a public realm."[59] But Niketown and its high-tech ambiance provides a fantasy environment premised on the very selfishness that people desire to escape. Niketown becomes Disneyland and consumerism becomes the real.

For Barber citizenship itself premises a public sphere.[60] Without a notion of public it is hard to imagine a democratic democracy because we are all just individual selves. The notion of 'the' public has always functioned as part façade. But the very façade of sharedness also functions as a promissory for the real. The tension is between our similar and common human needs and their specific and diverse manifestations. Without the notion of the public—of interconnectivity—there is no commitment to weave human bonds.[61]

The bourgeois nation-state was in part justified and authorized by the western/liberal-democratic version of publicness. This discourse, which is *also* a patriarchal and racialized discourse, has—often inadvertently—provided the tools for its own critique. The commonality of the public and the sharedness of citizenship allow those who are left behind to critique exclusionary and undemocratic notions of publicness and citizenship.

The racialized and engendered aspects of nation and its notion of public are exacerbated as the economic bourgeois nation-state is undermined by global capital and its cyber-media complex. Public/private domains are renegotiated in real and virtual space. The transnational sexual division of labor is highlighted against this backdrop even while it is not represented in the discourses of virtual reality. Girls, especially, are exploited in the global factory, with little recognition of the global facets of the patriarchal power of transnational capital.

As early as 1923 Walter Lippmann argued that there is really no such thing as 'a' public—it is a construction of politics. Government as "the will of the people is a fiction," the public "is a mere phantom." The phantom public is neither public nor informed, but rather "a bewildered herd." As a result, Lippmann put no great stock in what can be done by "public opinion" or the "masses."[62]

When the notion of public is positioned hostilely against difference and radical pluralism, it negates the possibility of a liberatory democracy. The problem of publicness also appears when the state governs corruptly rather than regulating and enhancing public space democratically.[63] A liberatory publicness must engage in open dialogue with multiple and different interests while protecting as well as empowering individuals within this domain.

Postcommunist states can also be privatized in the hopes of creating "public participation." The process of privatization in this case is to create a "civic morality" where individual freedom will flourish.[64] The goal of this participation is not merely to bring capitalist markets to eastern europe, but to use privatization to minimalize governmental authoritarianism.

This process may necessitate destroying and eliminating authoritarian governments while embracing the idea of publicness in new ways. A full democratization of public life means envisioning the needs of all people—especially girls and women across the color divide—while displacing the logic of consumer capital. This demands an assault against the racialized patriarchal discourses and practices of global capital and its privatized notion of the transnational state.[65]

New ways of thinking and imagining are needed to reclaim the idea of publicness. How does one establish trust and concerns across time and space? According to Anthony Giddens, this will require a "transformation of intimacy." After all, the nuclear plant disaster at Chernobyl demonstrated just how small the globe is.[66] Women from across the globe meeting in Beijing began to draw these new lines: of a public of women and girls across and through different cultures and values speaking against global poverty, sexual violence, and discrimination of all kinds.[67] This new notion of citizenship does not use the borders of nation/family, public/private, or government/economy.

As long as we are able to creatively imagine a community at odds with capital's use of racialized patriarchy, the very idea of publicness can be used as a start to discipline transnational capital.[68] This process of 'imagining' requires an assault on mediated, antigovernment imaginaries. The rhetoric of privatization—that government can do no right—distorts the possibilities available for creating democratic publics by assuming that all government, not just bad government, is the problem.

Actually, government largesse has a significant history of success. Through research and development, the u.s. government has funded fossil fuels and the "renewables revolution" with positive effects in developing energy alternatives, environmental protection, and a growth economy. Present cuts in research and development have a double-edged effect, especially in areas such as biofuels, bioenergy crops, and electric cars.[69] Many tools of government—including taxing, licensing, public works, and anti-trust laws—let individuals get what they want: parks to walk in, roads to drive on and so on.[70] It was government investment that put a man on the moon, footed the G.I. bill, and built Boulder Dam.[71]

The internet owes its life to government funding. U.S. corporate dominance in computers and software is due in large part to the pentagon's advanced research projects. Most of the computer technology used for the internet was developed by and for the military and now is being completely taken over by private corporations, as they reap the profits of public investment.

Today's continued privatization of the u.s. government means large cuts in social services and much smaller cuts in corporate welfare. The latter cuts are more indirect, but they nevertheless affect individuals by the air we breathe, the medicines that are not researched and developed, and so on. Similar cutbacks are part of most first-world politics today. Canadians took to the streets in October 1996 to demonstrate against the destruction of their governmentally subsidized safety net. Many regard this social safety net as quintessentially canadian, a defining component of their "caring society."[72]

The privatization of and cutbacks in the welfare state continue to devastate. By 1992, less than 1 percent of the u.s. GNP was spent on human welfare. By 1996, 20.8 percent of all u.s. children were defined as poor.[73] Yet, billions of dollars continue to subsidize corporate interests. Welfare caseloads shrink, homelessness escalates, and shelters overflow. Utter destitution is the order of the day in the streets of most large cities, while Wall Street bonus babies cruise the Hamptons in their shiny new muscle cars.[74]

Ending welfare as the united states has known it also kills the idea that we share a public responsibility for one another. The extreme forms of this new poverty constitute the other side of the process of privatization begun a quarter century ago. A new selfishness denies welfare benefits to immigrants and public education to the children of illegal immigrants.[75]

Nations point to the "limitations of the state" and the constraints of global capital to justify the abandonment of equality as a goal.[76] This abandonment creates new loopholes to help the very rich become even richer. It lessens capital investment in physical infrastructure, while those who have the means access services on the net.[77] Meanwhile, former chief of staff General Colin Powell, along with several former u.s. presidents, generate a campaign "to privatize compassion" through volunteerism in the corporate sector.[78] Good luck to us all.

It feels like I have settled between a rock and a hard place. We need to imagine and then claim a public-regarding politics that stands against BOTH global capital and a simple reactivation of previous forms of the social-welfare state. AND this dialogue must move toward a notion of publicness that embraces the needs of all people and their global environments.

Girls/Women's Publicness and Democracy

It is hard to think one's way through to a place, or space, or 'idea' of publicness that moves beyond the constraints of poverty, nationalist warfare, and postcommunist antigovernment rhetoric. But 'new-old' technologies can begin to map possibilities for imagining beyond the images of the new political and economic frontier that are served up for us. Tragically, just as telecommunications *could* hook up the world, no commitment exists to create the equality of access that could make this happen. Instead, new technologies rewrite and expand new inequalities on top of those that already exist.

A commitment to the needs of 'a' public is rooted in a notion of community that is derivative of *both* liberal and postcommunist democracy but moves beyond a simple mix of the two.

Instead, the concept of individual privacy is specified by the needs of girls/women of color and white women and rewrites the community at large through this stance. The space that is created from these imaginings is built by the people in it. Publicness becomes a "social product" in this process of definition.[79]

The process of thinking through to an idea of publicness that embraces individual privacy necessitates reimagining social responsibility. This reimagining must have as a cornerstone the full participation of women and girls of all colors in public dialogue. They must become part of the process that defines their needs. Abortion rights legislation would not be framed and decided upon by actors for whom the discussion is a mere abstraction. Instead, the different communities at risk would be at the heart of dialogue. Women and girls inside the global factory would set the stage for the discussion of a fair wage. Women of all colors would help set the priorities for breast cancer and AIDS research. Women across economic class divisions would initiate new progressive family legislation.

But does this leave us with selfish, interest-driven policy? No. Rather, it makes it possible for us to articulate policy for all the plural communities of the globe by specifying the plural realities—of race, sex, and class—that define any community. Also, if we contextualize the needs of individuals as part and parcel of a public orientation, then neither the individual nor the collective can be conceived without the other. The tension between diverse interests AND 'a' public are continually renegotiated in favor of a public that is *not* reduced to corporate interest as defined by its racialized and gendered structures.

The privatization of publics usually hits women of all colors the hardest because it is within public arenas that demands for equality—sexual, racial, gender—are heard, if they are heard at all. Private arenas, defined either as the family or the market, have not done well in addressing issues of equality. Gains toward equality, when they appear, have often occurred as a result of governmental action. A Black middle class developed largely as a result of civil rights struggles effected in government hiring and educational opportunities. Domestic violence, long hidden within family walls, was exposed by the women's movement and its critique of abusive family life. Resulting governmental legislation assumes an activist public responsibility for individual women's safety.

While the u.s. government shrinks from its commitment to address issues of equality, the number of media through which we can view, witness, and experience inequity has exploded. This increased exposure has mixed results. Print media, t.v., and the internet expose the problems, but they also allow us to escape them. We watch, but often we do not really *see*. This process of viewing but not really seeing defines new challenges to the creation of a deliberative and liberatory public life.

If cyber-media-corporate power continues to grow and national/governmental authority to shrink, the context for thinking about public life shrinks alongside it.[80] To whom do we direct our concerns? Who organizes dialogue? Toll-free phone numbers and computer menus already orchestrate too much activity today. Nobody is listening at the other end to hear your frustration. You can e-mail the White House whenever you like and pretend that it matters.

This is a mixed bag. On the one hand, all kinds of new possibilities now exist for an informed and participatory set of publics as people leave their bodies behind and travel in cyberspace. This ought to make one's color and sex irrelevant, but this is hardly the case. White men still dominate the airwaves and Jesse Helms is still protecting women and children from smut and abortion.

As the 'real' world becomes harder to live in, white flight to cyberspace accelerates. Cyberspace becomes to the nineties what the suburbs were to the fifties.[81] Although Al Gore believes the information highway can spread intelligence and participatory democracy around the world and likens the present possibilities to a "new Athenian age of democracy," he conveniently forgets that Athens was a slave society.[82]

Virtual reality both undermines *and* enhances the possibilities of a liberatory democracy that realigns the relations between family, state, economy, media, and globe to reimage a life of publicness rich in equality and privacy. These realignments must also negotiate the racial, patriarchal structuring of an earlier public/private divide and its media-ted representations. Herein lies cyberspace's enticing and maddening paradox.

Cyberpublics and Democracy

Information-age democracy assumes the power and centrality of computers. People will be brought closer to government through quick access to government documents.[83] Computer-aided ease allows for quick information, read as participation.

The digital nation creates new forms of communication. It allows for an online culture that lets people have "a genuine say in the decisions that affect their lives." It allows for new discussions in new ways with new ideas of civility. Whatever this new civility may allow, however, it remains exclusive. This new on-line culture is inhabited by young, educated, affluent, white males.[84] There is something less than new here. Not surprisingly, the mantra on the net is freedom, not equality. The net allows for new ways to communicate and to create relationships and communities.[85] Millions of north americans are faxing, e-mailing, and calling voice-mail boxes to speak out on issues. Tens of thousands of idiosyncratic websites and home pages now proliferate. This holds out promise for a publicness that stands outside the privatization demanded by global capital. And yet, cyberpublics will have to become much more inclusive for this promise to have any democratic reality.

Nevertheless, to a lesser extent, there is a new kind of "global plebiscite conducted on the behavior of nations" via the internet and e-mail and CNN. It is easier to see and communicate with faraway places.[86] Women in afghanistan use faxes and e-mail to let the world know what the religious fundamentalist Taliban is doing to them. Students at the University of Belgrade create a website to speak out against government censorship, sidestepping the state-controlled media. With only ten thousand internet users in serbia, students still hoped to tip things in favor of democracy.[87] Prodemocracy activists in china embrace the new access to unofficial news and uncensored information. Although the 'masses' are not yet online, prodemocracy forces hope to break the state's authoritarian hold on information. For these activists the net is a world unto itself, providing both escape and connection. "Digital islands exist" and promise change.[88]

These technologies allow for new ways of thinking, communicating, and knowing. This very same technology which promises to bring modernization to china may also undermine china's "monolith state itself."[89]

The weblike structure of information also contrasts with the hierarchical structure of u.s. military. The information capabilities pose an "information-war" threat that is "overwhelmingly unstructured." The u.s. pentagon fears a cyber equivalent of Pearl Harbor and is bracing for cybercombat.[90] But corporations will pay more for the best cyberminds, again giving global capital an advantage over traditional government.

Cybercommunications allow for new relationships across the globe. They often initiate information and scorn political authority and authorization. Cyberdiscourse can disassemble and reassemble established routes of order and control. In this sense, cybertechnology can enhance people's connectedness and concern with one another. It can create new ways of living publicly and democratically.

Yet, cybercommunications also reflect and are structured by old systems of power. Many poor people, people of color, white women, homeless children, africans, and others, are effectively excluded from the net. Without access there can be no participation.

Given the process of privatization in the u.s., new rules now strip billions of dollars of subsidies from telephone corporations operating in rural areas. This process will jeopardize the "nation's tradition of universal phone service."[91] Cheap rural phone hookups will stop being a right and become a privilege. Given that one needs a phone line to hook up a computer to the internet, information becomes a privilege too.

Maybe Umberto Eco's vision of democratizing cyberspace is a starting point for discussion. He wants the Bologna Town Council to build a town center with a public multimedia library, computer training center, net access, and a communal screen for individuals to share and see together. He proposes that the state guarantee net literacy as a basic right and build a "network of municipal access points."[92]

Cyberspace cannot be fully democratized unless the modes of information and production are constrained by and committed to a publicized notion of privacy. And the globe cannot be radically democratic unless, as Jean-François Lyotard writes, the public is given "free access to the memory and data banks."[93] The struggle of the twenty-first century is to control the new flows of cyber-media corporate power.

2
viewing

Media-ted Seeing and Cultural Capitalism

viewing

We come to know through a process of viewing. Most of us can only see what we can name. Though remarkably individual, seeing/viewing is a process that is also socially constructed. T.V. news tells us what is happening or has happened. Talk shows create/reflect what their viewers are thinking about. Newspapers choose what is news.

Media operates in the enlarged domain of language where the visual and spatial count for a lot.[1] The different components of mainstream commercial media—film, t.v., radio, music, theme parks, news, and publishing—simultaneously construct and reflect the corporatist culture that constitutes mass culture. This culture is consumerist and continuously redefines its patriarchal and racist underpinnings in order to develop new markets in the global economy. Consumerism utilizes identities along the margins—feminism, Black nationalism, gay rights—presenting us with ads featuring hip gay men, people in ethnic dress, or women in suits, for example. Meanwhile, the masculinist corporatist center holds sway. This re-imaging constructs a new postcommunist-corporate form of dominance.

Given all this, I query the 'new-old' relationships that create and maintain the symbolic culture of capital, the economic dominance of capital accumulation, the use of racist/patriarchal/sexual structures of oppression, and the media-tions that reproduce this nexus of power. I probe the ways in which the media and their cyberappendages negotiate the impotence of traditional bourgeois politics and the triumph of transnational capital. The triumph of this cyber-media-corporate complex is both real and not-real, propaganda and not-propaganda, true *and* false. The process is messy and contradictory and continually calls upon racialized and sexualized subtexts to develop new narratives. Media continually rescripts and realigns these post-cold-war developments.

Mass media largely defends the powers that allow consumerism to thrive.[2] Almost everything t.v. and tabloid media do is tied to marketing.[3] The public is transformed into consumers of media images and information rather than participants in political or cultural debates.[4] There is little new here— these issues preoccupied Walter Benjamin and Herbert Marcuse decades ago. What is different, however, is that telecommunications technologies allow for newly excessive layers of deceit and new possibilities for knowing. Scandal, almost always sexualized and racialized, becomes a kind of pop-cultural aesthetic in which corporate consumerism orchestrates new layers of deception.

My particular concern is how media, along with global telecommunications networks, are merging with the computer industry to reform the military-industrial complex of the 1950s into a media-ted information/cultural complex of incredible proportions. Disney and MCI are colonizing the internet. It is no surprise, then, that the main purpose of the Telecommunications Act of 1996 was not, as one might think, to regulate porn. Rather, its intent was to deregulate communication industries and thereby privilege market forces for the information highway.

Media-ting Consumer Culture

The control of communication, which is at the heart of media information in the global economy, has become more concentrated. Eight media conglomerates—including Randolph Hearst, Time Warner, and Rupert Murdoch's News Corporation—dominate the book trade.[5] Global media will soon be dominated by five to eight firms, NewsCorp, Disney, Time Warner, Viacom, and TCI. General Electric owns NBC; Westinghouse owns CBS; and Sony/Seagram owns MCA/Universal.[6] Westinghouse recently acquired American Radio Systems corporation for $1.6 billion, bringing 175 stations under its control.[7] With corporations owning most media outlets, access depends on pro-corporate standpoints.[8]

Thus, the distinction between real and media-ted erodes further.[9] In 1992 the u.s. Business Roundtable reported that an estimated $1 trillion (one in every six dollars of the GNP) was spent on marketing.[10] Marketing is intended to convince people to buy, to consume. T.V. programs, designed for particular segments of the population, are essentially sold to advertisers. Media become part of advertising as products are embedded in storylines and consumer items define media content.[11]

'Real' life is defined in and through consumption. A surreal intersection of media and product marketing create what Robin Anderson calls a "media environment." A harmony is established between advertising and media's content. Cause becomes effect, effect cause. The t.v. screen becomes the representation and justification for the consumer society.[12]

Communication in and of itself becomes a consumer activity. Mass media, as a main form of speech, fetishize consumption. Information does not inform or educate but rather distracts us from the real.[13] Reality exists here alongside its social construction and as a site of trauma. Media—as simulations of consumerist culture—continually reproduce the conditions of their own reproduction. For Umberto Eco, the so-called "vulgarity of the crowd" puts culture and its mass identification at odds with each other.[14]

The media that communicate and distribute fantasmatic information are semi-autonomous and semi-dependent domains of the structures of power. The media are not separate or apart from, looking at or into, the domain of power-politics. They are intimately involved in constructing corporatist information, but also offer us a lens on this process. And new telecommunication possibilities exist for both controlling and critiquing this process. This cyber-media-corporate complex must continually renegotiate the flux of global capital alongside its racialized and sexualized consumer markets.

The intimate *and* semi-autonomous nature of media-ted realities creates complicated negotiations among the nation-state, global capital, and consumer culture. Consumer culture also initiates and subverts aspects of racism and masculinism. This relationship does not mean that media are simply 'a function of' consumerism, because there is always a process of negotiation among these systems of power. This relative autonomy is occasionally enhanced by alternatives to the mainstream press and traditional broadcast media. New communications technologies—satellite dishes, the internet, camcorders—make possible more alternate voices as sources of news around the world, even though quite concentrated, become more porous.[15]

There are important reasons for challenging the very notion of a monolithic media as though it were a tangible, finite THING unto itself. It mislocates global capital's complex and multiple webs of media-ted power. When the media, as such, is targeted for undermining public trust, or faulted with challenging traditional values of family and nation, transnational capital and consumer culture get off scot-free. The media also acts as a decoy, as displeasure directed at the media detracts from the complex relations of power which structure it. For example, the notion that stopping violence on t.v. reduces violence on the globe misconstrues actual violence. Although this strategy *may* have some effect, t.v. violence is embedded in actual violence on the globe. The interdependence of these realms must be addressed before an effective strategy can be articulated.

There are other problems with a hate-the-media stance. The masses do not choose the owners of media corporations, nor do they choose the news anchors, reporters, or journalists. So when the media are treated as their own entity and blamed for creating cynicism and distrust, little political action follows. People complain about the media, which is quite different from changing them. Instead, media are left to operate with their multiple sources of power unnamed and unchallenged.

Hating the media offers a convenient deadend, particularly for those attempting to conceal the webs of power. Serbs interviewed about their notorious concentration camp in Omarska respond by denying the camp's existence and blaming the u.s. media for making it up: "There are no mass graves here. There was no camp—ever. . . . I blame the journalists. The Muslims paid the media, and the television pictures were forged."[16]

Because the media are not a homogenized edifice, there are cracks and fissures. Although most CNN reporting on the 1991 Gulf War was pentagon approved, this was not the only story told. Oppositional journalists and photographers were influential in uncovering the "triumph of the image" in the Gulf as part of a transnational capitalist agenda to establish a new world order.[17] However, given the near-monopoly control of information, this story was not told until months after the war, except via alternative satellite systems and video cassettes.

A different kind of story about a second Gulf War unfolded in February 1998. President Clinton and Secretary of State Madeleine Albright threatened to bomb the people of iraq if Saddam Hussein did not agree to a U.N. weapons inspection. A Clintonesque "town hall meeting" was organized for Columbus, Ohio, to build national support for the bombing. CNN covered the meeting live. But this time, without pentagon-approved reporting, dissenting voices and demonstrators in the audience were seen and heard around the globe. At the time of this writing, u.s. troops remain in the Gulf, along with previously imposed economic sanctions, but there will be no bombs.

The media, named as a coherent and homogenized thing, glosses over the structural aspects of its political/cultural activity. It misnames and misconstrues the structural web that connects transnational capital, nation-states, the patriarchal and racialized relations of these realms, AND their representation in and through t.v. news, newspapers, news magazines, t.v. talk shows, and call-in radio.

These media of discourse present, translate, expose, and cover up the tensions between global corporations and nation-based government. Media simultaneously protect hierarchies of power while also giving them visibility. This visibility is not predetermined in effect. Media mirrors can challenge the very systems of power of which they are a part. Media are both intimately constructed by corporate interests and the site of negotiation between the cross-pressures of nation and globe.

In this post-cold-war moment, media appear more protective of the corporate/consumerist realm than the public/governmental. We are continually told that capitalism is the new universal choice and can do no wrong and that government can do no right. Stories uncovering abuses by silicon breast implant makers, tobacco companies, and diet-pill manufacturers are never connected back to the ills of profit-making itself. So the public is informed that Dow-Corning knew all along that silicon breast implants were potentially dangerous to the health of at least some women, and that tobacco companies are/were complicit in trying to get young people to buy their addictive cigarettes. But this has little bearing on corporate capitalism itself. More to the point, there is little reason to believe that more vigilant government regulation, given the present nation-state, is necessarily the answer to such aberrations. Global capital is coated with teflon while first-world nation-state governments unravel.

Media's messages are packaged in continuous scandal. News and tabloid media undress President Clinton before our eyes while they discuss Paula Jones's charges of sexual harassment, Jennifer Flowers's story of her twelve-year affair with Bill, Monica Lewinsky's oral sex with the president, and Kathleen Willey's charges of unwanted sexual groping. We are asked to peep and pry while the nation becomes a tabloid.[18] There is also seemingly endless coverage of the misuses of power within the governmental arena, be it Whitewater, Irangate, or Travelgate. Little information is revealed, but government looks bad. It looks worse when Dick Morris, President Clinton's former advisor, resigns after being exposed for his long-standing liaison with a prostitute. Sexual scandal continues as an important subtext for the undoing and redoing of the first-world nation-state for global capital. In the case of Monica Lewinsky, the White House intern who supposedly had a sexual affair with President Clinton, we see how allegations of sexual misconduct create complicated screens of deception. After all, there is, as feminists argue, a politics to sex—the personal is also political—*and* there is also a distinction to be made between one's public and private life. There is also a difference between sexual harassment—defined with specific and narrow legal parameters— and stupid sexual misconduct, which is defined by vaguer cultural attitudes. The former has redress in the courts, the latter has none. Clinton is smart enough to know that "no means no," so he moves on to the next woman, while leaving a clear trail behind. It is not at all obvious how to always sort through this partially contradictory situation and media are clearly not interested in doing so.

Sexual scandal renegotiates locations of power while camouflaging the sources of power, as in the controversy over government funding in cultural arenas like the National Endowment for the Arts (NEA). In this instance, controversy over "scandalous" (read: sexually explicit) art was used to divert money away from the public sector. Similar distortions and confusions reappear. In the case of Kathleen Willey, a former white house volunteer/office worker, allegations of sexual indiscretion on the part of the President are equated with charges of sex harassment. *Sixty Minutes* airs Willey's interview and t.v. audiences get to hear about the sexual appetite of Clinton once again.

President Clinton's personal attorney, Bill Bennett, challenges the credibility of Willey and "all these women." The real victims here are the majority of women who need sex harassment law everyday to protect them in their jobs. Meanwhile, these "sexgates" resurrect the nation-state in postfeminist form. Although there is a politics to sex, Clinton escapes accountability through the confusion. His sex life is his own business and he will even use executive privilege to keep it so.

Yet, media never tell just one story. A large gulf separates mainstream news from alternative news, Hollywood from independent filmmakers. Many alternative media sources today operate alongside and in contrast to the mainstream news and documentary accounts.[19] And one need not always move to these more oppositional sources to find examples of the media undoing power. Exposés like the "pentagon papers" and Watergate helped expose the goings-ons of power. In the newest sexgate(s), corruption appears borderless, and it is not always clear where power is exactly located.

Of course, one wonders about the lasting effect of such exposure and scandal. Are we seeing too little too late? Is there too much disinformation to make these bits of information count for much? Is this truer today because the hierarchies of power are increasingly hard to name? These are keen problems if one hopes to develop democratic publics out of the process of exposing global capital's power across the globe.

Besides, mainstream media will fight the process toward democratization while they construct and distribute "reality." As an arena of power, the media manufacture their own protection through a fantasmatic array of stories that are only partial truths. The partialness always misrepresents the complex interrelations between consumer capitalism and its racialized/ sexualized meanings. Such information distorts more than it informs. Disinformation obfuscates and polarizes the intimate relationships between racism and sexism. In the Anita Hill/Clarence Thomas sexual harassment hearings and the O. J. Simpson murder trial, racism and sexual harassment/domestic violence were pitted against each other and used to obfuscate their interdependence. In both cases, the complex interrelations between sex and race were distorted. Clarence Thomas said the sexual harassment charges were part of a racist "high-tech lynching." O. J. Simpson pleaded innocent; his defense was a racist Los Angeles police department. For the most part, mainstream commercial media reproduced this story line.

The horrific police beating and sodomizing of Abner Louima in New York City was reported as a racial incident, with almost no discussion of the assault as a rape. The military sexual scandals starting with the Tailhook incident and ending at the Aberdeen base diverted attention from the complex structural nexus of militarist/masculinist racialized hierarchies of privilege. Partial lenses and viewings disconnect and distort the interrelations of consumer capitalism and its racialized/sexualized constructions.

The death of Princess Diana reveals the ultimate crassness of the media web of consumer markets and racialized patriarchy. Media simultaneously encoded patriarchal myth with new global consumer markets. Millions of dollars were spent while the globe mourned. Flowers were bought, magazines were sold, and memorabilia were produced. Meanwhile, the consumer frenzy refurbished the masculinist imaginary of a 'real' princess. She was royalty, but she was still an everywoman, suffering bulimia, a broken marriage, and problems with self-esteem.[20] Capitalist consumerism reused and refashioned the medieval patriarchal roots of a white european princess to reencode the multicolored globe. Beauty remains a white rich thing: Diana hugs and holds Black AIDS babies in Africa and speaks out against the maiming of children by land mines in the colored third-world-south, while the multicolored homeless sleep in the park that surrounds her home in Kensington Palace.

Media Mediating Political Culture

T.V. programs, newscasts, and call-in talk shows connect different groups—of people, identities, discourses—and also separate them. People bare their souls to complete strangers on talk shows, yet neighbors do not know each other. People can pretend to care about the world of t.v. screens while ignoring the world of their daily lives. Media corporations create the very parameters that silence the dialogue necessary for a democratized public life distinctly different from privatized consumerism. This is not to say that all talk-show discussion can be simply contained within these parameters, but the seepage has limited impact on the media-complex of power.[21]

Media allow us to not-see, which is different than simply blinding us. Viewings are already slanted. Skewed visions let us see and not-see at the same time. We may think we are seeing the whole picture when we are seeing only a small piece. News reports of israel, palestine, bosnia, and rwanda are depicted for millions through the lens of CNN. This opens the world to people across the globe, but it does so in absolutely western fashion. CNN privileges the news of the west against all the rest AND narrows news from within. It constructs "the west" in the process of reporting about it. Westernized conventions and codes are then appropriated and imitated by media elsewhere.

Media-ted reality infects the language that determines the 'real.' Discussion of drugs, sexual promiscuity, violence, teenage pregnancy, and 'welfare mothers' misrepresents and scapegoats youth and people of color.[22] 'Family values' campaigns are orchestrated by politicians who don't know the first thing about family commitment. The united states ranks first in child poverty within the industrial world, while the 'pro-life' movement focuses its energy on the unborn. News reports scapegoat so-called partial-birth abortions as an easy target, even though most doctors reject the terminology as inaccurate and grossly prejudicial. Timothy McVeigh's chief defense lawyer in the Oklahoma City bombing recognized early on that his 'media strategy' counted more than anything else.[23]

Media-ted reality misrepresents the complexities of the 'real.' Simple sound bites, rather than deliberative thought, dominate the airwaves: drugs, not poverty cause violence; welfare is bankrupting the united states (even though it makes up only 1 percent of the federal budget). The elimination of welfare will dump close to a million people into poverty because most of the children affected by the cuts live in families where the parent(s) already work.[24] Teenage motherhood is repeatedly distorted into a national epidemic even though teenage mothers give birth to fewer than 12 percent of all babies.[25]

If this is media's 'real,' then it is no surprise that Mickey Mouse can symbolize 'America.' He is a perfect icon because he is not real.[26] America, Jean Baudrillard argues, "is neither dream nor reality. It is a hyperreality. A utopia which acts like it is already achieved." As such, it functions like a "power museum for the whole world." The united states becomes a "giant hologram."[27] Burger King and Disneyland sum up the "mythic banality" and dream quality of a superficial corporatist culture defined paradoxically by profuse availability and enormous economizing and downsizing.[28] In the united states, where anorexia and overeating go hand in hand, everything SEEMS to become fantasy.

Communication becomes as exclusive as the consumerism it heralds. When information becomes a commodity itself, we have what Hans Enzensberger calls the "consciousness shaping industry," where electronic media with corporatist leanings re-define the real.[29] These media telecommunication transnationals hype consumerism to the exclusion of all else.[30]

Consumer culture and consumerism are woven through a notion of individualism that seduces everyone, the haves and have nots alike. Consumerism is equated with individual freedom. Transnational media representations construct consumerist culture as democratic—open, free, where anything is possible.[31] Its underbelly—poverty, hunger, and unemployment—remain uninteresting to mainstream media.

People are increasingly expected to be citizen/consumers, a new-old identity with a long history in u.s. capitalist culture. As transnational media corporations map new arenas of activity, divorced from geographical nations and linked to telecommunications networks, they seek to reframe their relationship to earlier first-world formations of the bourgeois nation. The cyber-media-corporate complex, with its racialized and masculinist structures, scraps the bourgeois imaginary of publicness and governmental responsibility. Citizenship is refetishized by global markets. Deliberative dialogue is avoided and even discouraged. Shopping is the preferred activity.[32] Freedom and opportunity displace commitments to economic, sexual, and racial equality. The global nation-state privatizes the public and downsizes democracy along with it.

In place of participatory democratic dialogue, media serve up a vaporized form of deliberation. So u.s. presidents—still white and male—must communicate rather than lead. They must sell their policies rather than convince. Clinton must show that he feels our pain, even as he orchestrates the policies that in part create it. To make us feel comfortable he becomes one of us, a mass consumer of MacDonald's hamburgers, Kentucky Fried Chicken, and Ford Mustangs. The consumer and the government merge in the form of the president.

This acknowledges the validity of the old cliché that politics has always been a con-game. Illusion, not substance, is what counts. T.V. presidents are about appearances, not ideas. Richard Nixon did not have to change; rather, he had to learn how to project a different image from what he 'really' was. A new Nixon was not needed, just a new media impression of him.[33] Daniel Boorstin calls this the "art of self-deception" and the demand for illusion, when image stands in for reality. In the end, there is only a "thicket of unreality."[34]

T.V. becomes a self-referential medium that merges news and advertising discourse. Infomercials merge real people and t.v. stars, stories and commodities, sports and product promotion.[35] The real becomes "media about media."[36] Bill Clinton appears on talk shows and the next day the news is about Clinton on *Larry King Live*. The increased media exposure of the president reveals little but becomes a shield of the real while it "appears to penetrate all masks."[37]

Much like virtuality itself, we seem to be served up copies of real people. Reality is simulated and illusory, so one begins to think nothing matters or that little can be done that will matter. This is great for transnational capital, which is left alone to masquerade around the globe. As we move toward reality as a "manufactured and metered commodity," it becomes harder to believe in democratic dialogue. Howard Rheingold calls these new relations of power a "reality-industrial complex."[38] Seeing is not about 'the' real or non-real; rather it obscures the distinction itself.

The united states is served up virtual democracy while the 'idea' of public responsibility for the communities one inhabits is undermined and challenged across the globe by the privatized commitments of global capital. At the same time, media telecommunications networks fantasize about global unity even as individual *and* collective options for imagining a rich and deliberative public life recede from view. In its place, the White House goes online with electronic mail to increase access to "the people." Things appear democratic while the hierarchical structures of consumerism intensify.

When u.s. media portray public life in a downward spiral of corruption and emptiness, they present politics as a depressing spectacle. This undermines the 'idea' that democratic publicness is either possible or desirable. James Fallows charges media with further undermining democracy through their own corruption, arrogance, and wealth. Star journalists seek their own fortunes rather than the truth and have become a part of the very relations they are supposed to expose. For Fallows the press has simply become a fourth branch of government.[39]

But it is not simply a fourth branch of government. It is an integral part of the new-old consumerist state with partial autonomy from the governmental realm. Because the u.s. government—as a geographical nation-state—is delegitimized by transnational capital, media are more closely aligned with the privatized politics of consumer culture than with the government per se. Media are therefore positioned somewhat uncomfortably between transnational capital's interests and the anachronistic constraints of a governmental apparatus not set up for twenty-first century global capital's needs.

Media only inadvertently disclose their own part in the structural mechanisms of power. Their interests are more likely to distort and distract than to disclose. This is why we need "an analysis of the analyzing class."[40] Those who watch need to be watched. There need to be reports on the reporters and on media's links with transnational capital and its racialized and sexualized underside. This would open up a public discourse on the excesses of global capital as a first step toward building alternate democratic visions.

Corporatist Domination and Telecom/Media Politics

Media, though implicated in transnational corporate interests, *also* have some autonomy in how they construct consumerist culture. This partial autonomy is rooted in the mechanisms of technology itself. New technologies such as VCRs, camcorders, answering machines, and computers provide a dynamic toward information access and control. Camcorders document what otherwise might not be witnessed, like Rodney King's beating at the hands of Los Angeles police. News reporters, as well as any individual who has access to a video camera, can show another side of any story. This creates new capacities for cover-up and deception, but also new possibilities for openness and exposure. In a somewhat different vein, the use of VCRs allows people more control over what they choose to watch or not watch. One can flick off a commercial and channel surf instead. Individuals can take more control over their own process of watching, even if they cannot change the menu of available choices.

This said, the corporate takeover of the airwaves is of critical importance to the politics of the day. Corporate mergers among telephone, cable t.v., and telecommunications systems are part of the attempt to control all electronic information delivery systems. The merger between Bell Atlantic phone company and Telecommunications cable empire has established a tight control over the production of video and informational programming. This corporate conglomerate now controls 42 percent of u.s. phone or cable lines entering homes.[41]

It should be little surprise, then, that broadcast media give large sums of money to congressional campaigns. Meanwhile, news broadcasters control whether and how members of Congress appear on t.v. In addition, Sprint Telenetwork donated $25,000 to the Clinton's 1996 presidential campaign.[42] These arrangements create significant silences.

Media conglomerates bespeak the intersections between news, entertainment, and telecommunications networks. Disney bought ABC, on the eve of the twenty-first century, in order to control more nonpolitical entertainment. Disney/ABC is more powerful and diversified as it locks up news and sports, radio networks, Disney Cable, home videos, theme parks, and so on.[43] General Electric acquired NBC around the same time in order to do much the same. Westinghouse has owned CBS for some time now.[44] Its commitment as a builder of nuclear plants and a main defense contractor has long set the contours for CBS News which are compromising at best.[45] These sorts of problematic alliances are increasing as the electronics industry, which has largely been subsidized by the federal government, is further privatized. The Telecommunications Act of 1996 fully authorized media corporations to compete for control of the internet, with barely a whimper made by Congress or the president.[46]

As a result of the Telecom Act, the net has been commercialized by a promarket ideology established by the cyber-media-corporate complex.[47] The internet is now colonized by private industry with its commercial rules and regulations. As early as 1980, IBM and ATT dominated the net, even though public dollars made the computer technologies of the net possible in the first place.[48]

The Telecom Act amassed unprecedented amounts of power for the few megacorporations that "control it all"—from t.v., movies, music, and publishing to print and electronic news.[49] The Act eliminates the barriers that separated telephone, cable t.v., and broadcasting.[50] Corporate interests are thus given a free hand for transindustrial mergers with the government's blessing. Telecommunications companies are now free to further colonize 'mass culture.'

This legislation was quietly ushered through by Al Gore. He argued on behalf of new rules and deregulations necessitated by the new needs of digital corporations. The Telecom Act legally institutionalizes the cyber-media-corporate complex, which is now free to dominate communication technologies. There was little congressional opposition.

The only public debate about the Telecommunications Act centered on the issue of pornography. The lack of a fuller debate is a prime example of how media-ted reality misrepresents the complexity of the real, and how governmental institutions replicate this process by responding to and constructing what is newsworthy. Although corporate capital was home-free with the Act, its particular paternalist patriarchal relations were yet to be clarified. So Senator Jim Exon sponsored what came to be called the Communications Decency Act, designed to protect the public, especially women and children, from the smut of the information highway. The free market of cyberspace would not be extended to pornographers. Patriarchal protectionism won this round. Children would be protected from the perversity that was just a few clicks away on their computers. "Any comment, request, suggestion, proposal, image or other communication which is obscene, lewd, lascivious, filthy or indecent" would have been punishable.[51] Debate and revision of the CDA continues.

Government intervention is enlisted to police the morality of the airwaves, while private corporate interests are permitted to police themselves. This protectionist stance toward children's exposure to porn cloaks and misrepresents the government's dismal record on taking responsibility for its children. In yet one more diversionary tactic, one is left to believe that the greatest harm children face in this transnational corporate globe is smut, rather than hunger.

The state polices rather than assists. This contradictory stance—of interventionist moral absolutism articulated alongside statist privatization of social welfare policy—is hardly new.[52] Jesse Helms and Henry Hyde—long-time pornography, gay rights, and abortion rights foes—have also extended the censoring and regulating of indecent speech on the net to information about abortion. This notion of 'indecent speech' finds its ideological precursor in the Comstock Law (1873) banning mail "of an indecent character."[53]

The paternalist moralism of Helms, Hyde, and others links porn to abortion. Each becomes symbolic of the other; both point to the loosened controls of the traditional patriarchal family. Both porn and abortion loosen the gender divide by publicizing sexuality. Paternalist protectionism—as fantasmatic as it is—seeks to reencode traditional gender roles, even though global capital demands otherwise. This tension—between traditional patriarchy and global capital—continues to challenge the parameters of the free market of the internet.[54]

However, Disney helps monitor the porn while the debate over censorship is inadvertently narrowed.[55] The censoring of information is not simply limited to porn in the first place. Information is already privatized by the networks that are available to online subscribers. IBM and Sears spent $1 billion on Prodigy—a computer service that censors all public postings— while the net is advertised as a completely open frontier by the corporate world and government alike.

The notion of a public concern for others is cleverly translated through the paternalistic patriarchal discourses that infantilize children and, indirectly, the women who parent them. Helms, Hyde, and even Clinton pretend that they live in a world where we 'really' care about one another, especially our children. This pretense necessitates V-chips that screen out violence, while transnational media corporations flood the markets of eastern europe with adult porn and beauty contests.[56]

Meanwhile girl-children slave away in maquiladora factories and in sweatshops in el salvador and taiwan. The politics of image, symbol, and simulacra rattle around in the hollowed-out verbiage of family-values rhetoric. At the same time, the megacorporations of consumerist culture are allowed their excessive greed.[57]

Of course, in the 1992 presidential election, Clinton promised to set the record straight. He would protect the hard-working middle class and give them their due. By 1996 it was clear that Clinton had forgotten most of his promises. And, most media do not help us remember since media's newest job is to have no memory.

The '96 Presidential Election as Chimera

As you read this, the '96 election is probably long forgotten. So let me make a record of the '96 election as a watershed in the media-ting of elections. Few people today think of elections as anything BUT media events. The '96 election, in particular, was a mix of amnesia and anesthesia.[58] This being the case, memory itself becomes subversive.

The slim majority of those who still vote sleepwalked through '96. The election orchestrated the normalization and acceptance of 'no choice' discourse as part of the electoral arena itself. By the time of the 'virtual' debates in October '96, election rhetoric had cleansed itself of all controversy—about abortion, welfare reform, health care, and global competition. There were 'choiceless choices' to be made. This hollowed-out model of national politics further smooths the way for transnational capital.

Variations of capital's sexist and racist policies cover over the lack of 'real,' substantive choosing. Dole said he did not favor family leave; Clinton said he did. Neither candidate said the leave should be with pay, which is the only way to give it any 'real' effect, especially for women.

No simple linear process has landed us here. Rather, there has been a complicated nonlinear process of delegitimizing the role of government as a major player in creating a cohesive nation. Since 1989, we have seen a rhetorical unifying of the globe as capitalist, with no real alternative or choice. Focus on the sexual/private side of elected officials misrepresents the entirety of politics. Our minds have been numbed through continual scandal. Conflict is continually neutralized by Clinton's endless set of compromises.

So we have politics as pretend. Politics as performance. Politics as sound bite. Politics as chimera. But this screen is not one and the same as its symbol. The '96 election was not about nothing. There are real needs not being met. There are real people who are homeless, and hungry, and in need of health care, and seeking abortions they cannot obtain.

The '96 election silenced these concerns and instead presented a Democrat and Republican, neither of whom embrace public debate and dialogue, although Clinton pretends to. Both are neoconservative/neoliberals attempting to find a power base.[59] One swings to the right; the other to the center. Neither is anywhere close to a liberal democrat, even though Clinton is ironically smeared with this label while capitulating to right-wing demands.

Liberalism has become hyperreal.[60] It is a code word for (pseudo)socialism. The label, as code, no longer relates to any actualized meaning. It has taken on its own significance and political history and is used to smash democratic imaginings that were once aligned with it. It is the late-twentieth-century equivalent of "red" or "commie," and it is similarly misapplied.

ON PRIVATIZATION IN '96

Neoconservatism has been attacking and downsizing the social welfare part of the nation-state for about a quarter-century now. Not much is left, especially since the signing of the welfare reform/destruction act. This privatization of the public arena—the rejection of the symbolic community with its tired and its poor—is the underside of corporate excess.

Privatization takes many forms. What used to be done by the government will now be done by private corporations. Privatization defines individual responsibility as the core of the opportunity society. What was once thought of as public is now private. Society is privatized by greed and isolation.

The other side of this privatization of publicness is that it reduces the private realm—be it corporate interests or sexual privacy—to public life. In this reduction, sex scandal stands in for knowledge. Instead of connecting private/personal life to a public set of meanings, personal/private stories—like the hooker foot fetish of Clinton's former media advisor Dick Morris or the supposed affair with Monica Lewinsky—parade as information in the disinformation society. Supposedly, we know it all, even the sexual. But we dismiss these stories as not real politics, as something else.

Maybe one reason the public seems so curious about sexual scandal is that it seems like the only 'real' thing left in politics. Or as Russell Baker says, thank heavens for sex, "thank heavens for politicians who never learn. At last, life!"[61] So sex is not irrelevant here, nor is it simply image making. Rather, it reveals the 'realness' of image making as part of the deception itself. By 1998, however, there may be too much talk of sex and too much reality. Nevertheless, Clinton's approval ratings climb in spite of all the revelations of sexual impropriety.

ON GENDER GAPS/CANYONS IN '96

Strangely enough, women supported Clinton by anywhere from 12 to 25 percent more than men. This is true for middle-aged women more than younger women, black women more than white women. Because he is raising a daughter, Clinton was 'seen' as more caring than Dole, more in touch with the world, gentler and kinder. Dole was skewered as the nasty husband who dumps his wife. So angry white men were ready to vote for Dole, while "anxious white women," especially so-called soccer moms who live in the suburbs, were courted by Clinton's campaign.[62] These mainly white, married, college-educated women who work part-time became the symbol of the struggling middle class.[63]

News media cannot treat women seriously even when they are trying. Thus, stressed and hard-working white women who live in the suburbs become "soccer moms," and this group stands in for the diverse women's vote. Women of color, poor women, professional women, and pro-choice women had nowhere to go other than to hang with the Clinton camp, so they did not need to be courted. These women had to swallow the way Clinton dumped Zoe Baird, Johnnetta Cole, Lani Guinier, and Joycelyn Elders. And they were expected to forget about Gennifer Flowers and Paula Jones too.

Many progressive women were not excited about Clinton or the Democrats but stuck with them, while white men, excited or not, moved toward the Republican party. Polls show that the real gap between men and women concerned the existence of the social welfare state and the expansion of health care, social programs, and affirmative action. This explains why white men favored the Republican party in the '94 election by 26 percentage points while unmarried women—of all colors—backed Democrats by a 32-point margin.[64]

Women are concerned with family issues like health care and education. But they are also twice as concerned as men about the insecurity of their finances.[65] Many more women than men still believe in an activist government that provides a social safety net.[66] Given many women's economic vulnerability this comes as no surprise.[67]

Clinton said he would keep abortion legal. He stands by a woman's right to choose, but he forgets about creating access. Abortion has been individualized like much else: it exists for those who can get it, and the government has no role in creating opportunity either in terms of available services or in funding for the poor.

Clinton utilized his pro-abortion record and his support for the abortion pill RU-486 to capture the women's vote. His pro-choice stance covered up much of his centrism/neoconservatism. Many of his federal court appointees have been pro-choice, but otherwise not 'liberal.'[68]

I can't help feeling uncomfortable about women being a decisive factor in the election of a man who clearly loves the sexual politics of conquest. He feels our pain and gets off on the cheap. His stance on abortion allows him lots of room to maneuver. Faye Wattleton, former president of Planned Parenthood, notes that abortion has become a proxy for a lot of other issues women care about.[69] Clinton's abortion stance lets him look like a moderate while he oversees the orchestration of the neocon/neoliberal state. Women can have the right to decide about their bodies while the safety net is pulled out from under them.

In this whole process, things are not what they seem.[70] Clinton is feminized—he diets and worries about his weight. Meanwhile, Hillary is masculinized as the ball-busting policy wonk. In the beginning, in 1992, there was much upset about Bill's philandering and lack of real backbone. Hillary was an asset then. She spoke on his behalf and defended their marriage for all to see. And he used her unspoken feminism to shield himself.[71] They mimicked a fashionable androgyny.

Four years later, the public seemed exhausted or anesthetized by it all. And women, more than men, sided with Clinton as the choiceless choice. This is quite a sorry state: women preferring someone who looks and sounds *like* he cares to someone who does not know how to look *like* he cares.

Somewhat expectedly, Hillary landed in the doghouse. She absorbs the attacks and leaves Bill free to seem more presidential. Hate Hillary, as we are often directed to hate the mother and wife. But who really dislikes her? And why? Is the criticism of Hillary because she is corrupt, like so many people in power? Or is it because she is a strong woman when she is supposed to be just a wife?[72]

In this surreal arena of politics, Dole cast about looking for female voters. The two parties seemed to be gender swapping. The Republican convention appeared feminized with Lizzie Dole working the crowds and Susan Molinari with baby in hand. Those watching were not supposed to pay any attention to the fact that Molinari's vote matched Newt Gingrich's over 90 percent of the time. Columnist Maureen Dowd called the convention an "estrogen festival to woo women."[73] Meanwhile, the Democrats acted tough, like the stern father, vowing to clean up welfare.

Of course, by 1996 many already knew that political conventions are made for t.v. They are orchestrated and rehearsed, as even the media analysts acknowledge. Nevertheless, people act as though the chimera matters. Inevitably, however, fewer and fewer are listening and watching.

Politics is said to be the activity of image making by the image makers themselves. T.V. programmers expect the public to pretend. So, by the time Dole took center stage at his convention, all controversy was left behind. This was most true of the mess he made of the abortion issue. After dropping the tolerance plank of pro-choice Republicans, both pro-choice and anti-choice voices were quieted at the convention. Only Colin

Powell uttered the word "abortion."[74] After that, it was dropped as an issue for the remainder of the campaign.[75]

For the Democrats, abortion became a foil and operated as a mask for the destruction of social welfare programs. This is not to say that abortion is only a mask. But it was used this way in the '96 election, allowing Clinton to pander to the angry white male vote.[76]

In the end, abortion, family leave, affirmative action, welfare reform, and immigration law were silenced as an entire package.[77] These are the real issues, and an open dialogue and conversation would have uncovered the limited choice between Clinton and Dole. Instead, the orchestrated silences promoted a narrowed vision of privatized politics. With no clear enemy—like the former soviet union—liberalism, in its demonized form, becomes the 'communism' to fear.

Abortion—as a discourse of freedom of choice—takes on new significance today because it remains one of the few sites where the language of choice, not the market, has enormous pull. As such, it should locate pro-choice voters in a critical stance toward media-ted privatized politics.[78]

ON CHOICE AND GLOBAL CAPITAL IN '96

Antitax rhetoric is all of a piece with anti-government jargon. Clinton said he would end government as we have known it. Government tax structures, along with deregulation of land rights, pollution, patents, and so on, give capital a free hand. Meanwhile, antitax rhetoric is used to seduce struggling middle-class workers.

This antitax, antigovernment stance is a tough place to be as a politician. Neither Clinton nor Dole can speak of a government that entitles people to what they need without challenging the very business interests that back them. This is no small consideration when a presidential campaign costs $800 million. It is no surprise that even one of Dole's advisors found it hard to clarify how the two candidates differed. He said of the Clinton camp, "they're running to the right of us."[79]

The presidential debates institutionalized the 'no-choice' discourse of global capital for all to see. And the extreme right-wing politics of the militias keep the neocon/neoliberals of transnational capital looking centrist. These are not happy alternatives: neocon/neoliberals at the center and radical rightist anti-abortionists and militias in the wings.

ON REFORMING/DESTROYING WELFARE IN '96

Clinton's attitudes toward welfare are an intrinsic part of his privatized 'New Democrat' stance to end government's public responsibility. This is actually quite similar to his policy stance while governor of Arkansas.

The destruction of social welfare involves cutting $56 billion in state support.[80] Clinton justified his position: "On balance this bill is a real step forward for our country, our values, and for people who are on welfare." He also admitted disappointment that "the bill contains provisions that will hurt legal immigrants in America, people who work hard for their families, pay taxes, serve in our military." But in the end, he said, the bill would help those who are "trapped on welfare."[81]

The welfare legislation Clinton signed into law, derived largely from Newt Gingrich's Contract With America, ends the government's guarantee of cash assistance for poor children. The head of every family on welfare has to work at a job within two years. Lifetime welfare benefits are limited to five years. Payments to unmarried teenage parents under age eighteen are allowed only if the mother stays in school and lives with an adult. Eligibility standards for disabled children are much stricter.[82] For the first time since the New Deal, no guaranteed help from the government exists for the poor. States are free to develop their own measures, no matter how severe.[83]

Little is said of the fact that creating enough entry-level jobs for the poor would take twenty-one years at the current rate.[84] Little is said of the tax breaks given to corporations and wealthy individuals in 1996, amounting to $440 billion, more than seventeen times the combined cost of state and federal spending on AFDC (Aid to Families with Dependent Children).[85]

Welfare functions as the imaginary of failed government and poor women of color as the scapegoats. Most families who need welfare usually need it for less than two years at a time. About 40 percent of these families are on welfare for one year at a time; another 28 percent leave welfare within two. For these families, welfare is not a trap but an aid for those who work jobs at poverty wages.[86]

The 'typical' family on AFDC is a mother and one child. In stark contrast to the imaginary welfare woman who has babies at the expense of the government, the birthrate among AFDC women is lower than among the rest of the population. And more to the point, the welfare payments themselves have become more imaginary (as a hand-out) than real.[87]

Making social welfare look bankrupt is one strategy of wearing away at the 'idea' of government responsibility for its public(s). The government is blamed for creating the very problem of poverty it is supposed to redress. Depict the poor as irresponsible and lazy, and presto, they become irresponsible and lazy. Senator Patrick Moynihan is clear about how corrupt this is. The author of the infamous Moynihan Report of 1965, which attacked the government's role in maintaining the deviancy of single-parent Black families, today stands against the abolition of social welfare because it will plunge at least another 2.6 million people into poverty, 1.1 million of those being children. "Just you wait until there are a third of a million children in the streets," threatens Moynihan.[88]

This elimination of welfare for the poor—under the guise of reform—paves the way for new business opportunities as private companies compete to take over the administration of welfare. Leading the way is Ross Perot's $12.4 billion information-technology company Electronic Data Systems.[89]

ON UNMASKING CLINTON IN '96

So who is the 'real' Bill Clinton? What is the 'media real' here? Remarkable as it may seem today, Clinton was elected in 1992 promising health care for all. In his 1994 State of the Union message, Clinton held up a pen and told congress that he would veto legislation that did not guarantee every american health insurance that could never be taken away. Health care, he said, was "our most urgent priority."[90] This stance was abandoned without pretense in 1996. Clinton's most aggressive stance in the '96 election consisted of his professed need to determine "ways to give more people access to health insurance,"[91] and of his guaranteeing new mothers an extra day in the hospital. Meanwhile, 40 million people remain without health insurance; medical insurance companies orchestrate the movement toward managed/mangled care; and the private market is remaking the health care system according to its needs.[92] Mainstream media colluded in these erasures.

Clinton also supported the Marriage Act, which denied spousal social security and pension benefits to gays. He supported the V-chip and the Communications Decency Act. He says he is against discrimination of gays in the workplace, but apparently he views this as an entirely different issue from discrimination by marriage law.

While Clinton supports policing porn on the internet, he leaves in place catastrophically disproportionate sentencing for crack and cocaine use. He has overseen a crime bill that created dozens of new capital offenses. He supports the idea of random drug testing for welfare recipients, and the welfare bill he signed denies assistance to anyone convicted of a drug felony. He supports net censorship, wiretapping, and file gathering.[93] He believes that civil liberties must be amended in the fight against terrorism. Even his support of a minimum wage increase to $5.15 an hour still leaves a family of four below the poverty line.

He allowed a weakening of the Delaney Clause, which monitors the carcinogens in our food. He has lessened the effects of the Endangered Species Act. He has pushed to privatize public lands, continued to allow the devastation of western forests, and overseen the exacerbation of chemical pollution.[94] He refused to sign the international treaty banning land mines. This antitobacco prochild president killed a bipartisan measure to increase cigarette taxes as a source of subsidy for poor children's health care.[95] Once again, there is little media representation of this profile.

Given this record, Clinton and Dole don't seem all that different. Yet, Clinton is still seen as a liberal by 37 percent of those polled, and another 43 percent see him as a moderate.[96] Clinton nurtured this moderate/liberal identity as he stood up to the gun and cigarette lobbies at the Democratic convention.

Clinton has retained a commitment to affirmative action. He says we must "mend, not end" it, although the process of mending may undermine its initial integrity. Clinton has also appointed more white women and members of minorities to high-level positions than any other president.[97] These concessions to liberal feminists and civil rights activists sustain the 'moderate/liberal' rhetoric. Media are pretty active constructing this image.

After Clinton's victory in the '92 election, many hoped that he would make a difference, that he might turn back the Reagan-Bush decade of privatization. That did not happen. The '96 election left a residue of mixed signs. Clinton nearly repudiated all the important ideas of the Democratic party, becoming by default a New Democrat. Hope is harder to come by now. Instead, progressive, feminist, civil rights, pro-choice, labor, gay, immigrant, and child's-rights voices must be organized and heard as loud, or louder, than the selfish voice of transnational capital. This necessitates, in part, a struggle to democratize media and with it public life.

Imagining Media Democracy

Media produce, reproduce *and* reflect culture and thus are part of the culture industries. These industries continually renew the foundations of consumerist culture by remaking the sexual, gender, and racial symbolic order. Consumer culture is then integrally formed through transnational capital, but in deference to the racist/patriarchal hierarchies of the globe. Even when the media pay homage to indigenous cultures in the middle east, south asia, and the caribbean, they do so through their hegemony. Transnational corporatism builds and rebuilds its racialized and masculinist glass ceilings.

With the demise of the imagined 'public' in north, south, east, and west, media take over this space. T.V., movies, and music make noise and pictures, mimicking a world for us to connect with. This process—of experiencing the world we live in through media-ted viewing—reframes the relation between public and private lives.

Media repackage the divisions between publicness and privacy in part by displacing the democratic promissory of public regardingness with market/consumer individualism. Media, as the expressions of consumerist culture, refocus activity to individual experience. The individual becomes self-sufficient according to market ideology. But there is an interesting twist here. If privacy is determined in relation to publicness and there is no public, then privacy becomes something other than what it has been. The idea of privacy is conceived in relation to its tension with public life. Because patriarchal privilege has been negotiated and structured through the public/private divide, post-cold-war formations between corporate media interests and nation-states require a realignment of these spaces. It is not at all clear that privacy can have the same saliency it has had if there is no public space to enter. Who needs privacy if you are all alone to begin with?

Nevertheless, media lenses continue to reproduce the public/private divide, even as they dismantle aspects of it. So, patriarchal privilege mainstreams men and marginalizes women but the locations/spaces of this process are changing.[98] As the governmental/public arena is undermined, we will see more women occupy 'public' sites. Madeleine Albright, the first woman secretary of state, may be the first in a long line of firsts. This may be the twenty-first century's twist on old forms of male privilege: women will occupy downsized sites of power while their numbers increase in the global labor force.

Consumer culture and transnational capital wish to govern themselves in the twenty-first century. And it looks more and more like governments, including the u.s. government, are accommodating this need. They are supposed to look like they govern, to become a copy, to appear real. Even government officials argue that governmental functions, be they air traffic control, mail delivery, or running the public schools, should be taken over by private industry. So governing has become more an activity of signs that allow 'the' public to think that there is governing going on, like the Wizard of Oz behind the curtain.

News media are key to this process. They continually report on the activities of government officials even as they reveal the signs as a sham. So we are led from one scandal to another with no effect. Clinton is charged with sexual harassment, his friends in the Whitewater affair are found guilty, Hillary finds long-lost papers on a table in her private quarters and says she does not know where they could have been—and Clinton goes on governing.

This does not bode well for reclaiming the public sphere for democracy, in either its virtual or real formations. But there is a difference between virtual and real, between democracy and hyperdemocracy. CD-rom pioneer Bob Stein makes this very clear. He believes that the middle class, instead of having nice homes, cities that work, and subways that run, will have virtual worlds and will live in their computers. When they want to return to the inner city and lay eyes on people of color, they will do so through mass-marketed music, videos, films, sitcoms, and virtual reality crime news programs. In the meantime, the truly rich will have the real stuff. Bill Gates's $50 million mansion is *decidedly* real.[99]

To build a democratic vision of public life we have to believe in something beyond the self and its consumptive needs, beyond the privatization of the globe. So we must become wildly optimistic before we can think our way ahead to a media committed to democratic practices.

Because we see through media, they must radically reorient themselves toward invigorating a dialogue committed to publicness. This publicness must recognize the multiple needs of the communities it represents, and it must do this without reducing individuals to a mean-spirited individualism. Instead of a gender/racialized hierarchy, the pictures we see must depict the full diversity of communities. And those who speak and provide dialogue must do so, not from a singular identity, but from multiple and conflicting orientations.

When the news reports on bosnia, we must hear croat, serb, and muslim voices, each in their male and female tones. When it reports on israel, we must hear news of palestine and the multiple identities residing on each side of the divide. When it reports on the Gulf War, we must hear iraqi women and soldiers, and u.s. troops: black, white, chicano, male and female.

Oppositional media initiate this process. Out of the mainstream, outside the major networks, alternate visions of the real and possible are offered.[100] But these voices must become louder, more visible, and more widespread. The New York Free Media Alliance (NYFMA), in calling for a democratic media and democratic society, demands an end to "the weapons of distraction," a repeal of the Telecommunications Act of 1996, a stop to the spectrum giveaway, and a return of the airwaves to the public.[101]

Democratic media require open dialogue and discussion, as well as access to technologies for production and distribution. Imaging diversity is not enough. Global capital must be exposed as an obscene system. This means moving beyond consumerist culture and transnational capital to a vision of democratized publics. It remains a crucial question whether the new technologies of cyberspace will be able to unleash this process.

3
talking

Cyberfantasies and the Relations of Power

talking

I use the term 'cyber' to refer to computer-mediated activity[1] AND the discourse that masks the relations of power embodied in and structuring these activities. Cyberspace, with its technological innovations of the internet and e-mail, allows for new interactive and dialogical styles AND the cyber-media-corporate complex utilizes this promissory to mask its role in delimiting much of this democratic capacity.

Cyberspace creates new possibilities for democratic process: new publics are created across time and space; online access to elected officials develops; access to infinite amounts of information increases. Fresh possibilities now exist for a liberatory politics. Yet, because cyberspace is already colonized by corporatist interests, preexisting racial, sexual, and gender inequalities are complexly rewired.

Cyberdiscourse thus presents an epistemological stance toward information and its relation to transnational capital that

70

obfuscates the realities of exploitation and domination in the global economy. Cyberdiscourse operates as a democratic imaginary alongside that of the fantasmatic open globe. Supposedly, neither cyberspace nor the globe have a center of power. Neither are defined by local borders. Both represent new democratic comm*unities* defined by unfettered individual freedom.

Cyberdiscourse utilizes an episteme defined by digital information that privileges the autonomy of technology. Cyberdiscourse articulates an epistemology that justifies the cyberspaces it creates. It thus becomes a perfect decoy for obfuscating the realities of global capital with its sexual and racial hierarchies of privilege.

Each time someone uses a credit card to buy food, gas, or get cash, they enter cyberspace. These computer-run interactions save time and create ease for the consumer. However, workers at these same locations—food stores, gas stations, and banks—are surveilled by the very same machines. Their keystrokes are numbered, their every activity—from duration of transaction to bathroom break—monitored. One's class positioning as a worker is structured by cybertechnology, just as technologies have always displaced the control of labor. Even though many of these same workers, as consumers, use credit and money cards themselves, as workers they are pitted against these cyber expressions of power/control.

What, then, are the power relations in cyberspace? Between transnational media and telecommunications corporations AND the rest of the globe? Between producers and consumers of computer-mediated reality? Between government and intraclass corporate interests? Between patriarchal privilege and global capital? Between racialized hierarchy and global flows? Each of these relationships is complex and multiple. There are many different kinds of consumers, and identity is always plural.

Cyberspace appears to exist everywhere. Yet, it is almost nowhere to be found in poor and rural areas, whether a country be poor or rich. This fantasy cyberglobe poses an interesting contradiction. On the one hand privileged members of western 'techno-service-information' societies embrace the new mechanical/electrical capacities that supposedly allow them to interact with people anywhere. Meanwhile, much of africa, let alone western countries, is left out of this imaginary community. AND, although cybercapacity, like e-mail and internet access, hooks up people in parts of the globe that would otherwise be completely left out of the mix of western chatter and culture, many of these people live in a real world that starkly contrasts with the glitz of cyberinformation.

The American Dream exported via global telecommunications networks acts as a western promissory and democratic vision for the globe. This imaginary instigates significant yearnings on the part of people in such countries as china and russia, all the while smashing democratic possibilities, which are quickly smothered by the new exploitative capacities of digital technology. Workers in indonesia, thailand, and mexico toil in sweatshops at substandard wages for transnational corporations that enrich themselves online. However, these workers of the new and larger capitalist-created communities also begin to agitate for better conditions fed by the global imaginary itself.

Information Haves and Have-Nots

Cyberspace is accessible to only a small fraction of people outside the west. Eighty-four percent of computer users are found in north america and northern europe. Sixty-nine percent are male, average age thirty-three, with an average household income of $59,000.[2] The top twenty internet-connected-computer countries are significantly homogeneous. They are first-world, except for singapore. Finland leads the list, followed by iceland, the united states, norway, and australia, with sweden, switzerland, and the netherlands not far behind. One-third of finland's people carry mobile phones, many of which have e-mail and World Wide Web (WWW) access.[3]

The racial elitism of cybercommunities is palpable. In the united states, only 20 percent of African-Americans have home computers, and a mere 3 percent subscribe to online services.[4] Rather than a highway, the internet seems like a segregated private road. This newest form of "white flight" has white men retreating to their computer screens. In the 1950s, highways connecting the city to the suburbs were built to allow escape. In the 1990s it is digitized wiring.[5]

Approximately 80 percent of the world's population still lacks basic telecommunications access. Nevertheless, more than 160 countries outside north america and western europe have links to the internet, with some 20–30 million users.[6] Asia has 1.5 million users, two-thirds of whom are in japan. There are more telephone lines in Manhattan than in all of subsaharan africa. The united states has thirty-five computers per hundred people; japan has sixteen; taiwan has nine. Ghana, on the other hand, has one computer per thousand people.[7] In france, where there has been open hostility to the global market fewer than 15 percent of homes have PCs and fewer than 1 percent of them are connected to the internet.[8]

The infrastructure of information technology is spotty at best. Nearly fifty countries have fewer than one telephone line per hundred people. In bangladesh, a computer costs as much as half a year's average salary, and a modem costs more than a cow.[9] In china, PCs priced at $2,000 are more than four times the average urban annual income of $480. The PC, modem, software, and monthly access fee needed to access the internet remain out of reach for most.[10] Only 150,000 chinese—barely one in ten thousand—are actually wired. On average, there are seventeen chinese for every phone line.[11]

In contrast, 35 percent of u.s. families have a PC at home, and 30 million people were online in 1997.[12] This means that about 11 percent of u.s. households subscribe to an online service, and about 16 percent have modems.[13] Many people still cannot afford a computer and the twenty-dollar monthly access fee. Electronic information constructs an information hierarchy—of haves, have-nots, and have-lates—which mediates access, privilege, and power.[14] Nevertheless, 66 million users are projected for the year 2000.

Cyberdiscourse fashions an imaginary vision of an interconnected world that is only part true. The phrase 'World Wide Web' images the world about as accurately as the baseball phrase 'The World Series.' In the latter case, only u.s. baseball teams compete. In the former case, only about 40 percent of the world's population even has daily access to electricity.

In spite of the inequity, and maybe even because of it, cyberspace functions as a new imaginary location of escape, promise, and profit. Cyberspace becomes a whole new arena to conquer where privatization openly seduces some, but silently punishes those who are excluded.

Cyberimaginings allow communication with people in other countries, while one's neighbors can be ignored. Speech takes place between people who have no initial responsibility for one another.[15] New rules define the modes of interaction. E-mail allows one to communicate with others on one's own terms, according to one's own needs of time and availability. One can ignore e-mail correspondence, respond at will, send and receive messages at any time. E-mail also allows mobile populations easy connection to their original homelands, a kind of alternative homeland and multiple identity.

Corporate and government voices relentlessly hype the internet. Clinton and Gore repeat, mantra-like, their commitment to internet availability and access. Meanwhile, poverty rates soar and much of the working poor are forced to rely on understocked food pantries to feed their families. Public schools and public libraries are downsized along with the tax base that once subsidized the purchase of computers at these locations.

It could cost upwards of $100 billion dollars to wire and equip u.s. schools. Clearly this is a boondoggle for computer corporations, but it is less clear if computerization is what public schools today need most. Studies are beginning to challenge the relationship between cognitive skills and computer use. Some educators argue that there is a loss of creativity and cognitive development as a result of learning through computer programs. These educators say that class size should be reduced and teacher's salaries be increased before students go online.[16]

Conflicting interests between cybertech and people's access mirror the tensions between the profit motive and people's needs. The transnational corporate commitment to privatization stands in stark contrast to the seductive democratic technological potential of computer-mediated dialogue. Online anonymity can challenge and/or displace established sexual/racial hierarchies; gender swapping can liberate teenagers from traditional sex-role expectations; cyberskills can reposition people in the world; e-mail can sidestep authoritarian regimes. Obviously, the outcome of this struggle—between transnational capital's control of telecom/cyber networks AND the democratic potentials of cybertechnology—is not yet decided.

Class Structure and the Info Society

The telecom/cyber corporations in the united states have launched a full scale initiative to rewire the country. A first step in this process is to justify the wiring as necessary for everyday practices. This is made easier by the fact that computers are already embedded in everyday life. Tiny crash-proof computers repeatedly assist consumers. Microprocessors facilitate money and phone cards, calculators, kitchen equipment, and so on. The internet as an infrastructure of sorts creates a techno/socio-structure of everyday life that appears quite normalized and necessary.[17]

The imaginary of cyberspace fits neatly alongside transnational capital's needs, which are nurtured by global telecommunications. Cyberspace attaches new significance to high-tech information. Digital technologies detach information from the physical plane while designating a new language. Digital data store information in numerical codes, as disembodied knowledge.

According to William Mitchell, infobahns deliver bits of information in ways that entirely change the world as we have known it.[18] The new accelerated automation processes electric language in digital form. For Michael Heim, the word processor has become the calculator of the humanist.[19] Information takes on new forms that are interactive and multiple. Knowledge is webbed and networked through electronic linking.[20]

Information gets defined as a form of intellectual capital and the new source of power. The "knowledge workers," according to business mogul Walter Wriston, control intellectual capital. They will "carry the means of production in their brains." They are the new bourgeoisie because information technology made information the most important factor of production. In this scenario, the pursuit of wealth is the pursuit of information.[21]

Information is said to be power. But information does not float freely. It remains tied to a web of power that structures the production and distribution of information. Information, stored in disembodied digits, retains its relational ties to human labor even though appearances might suggest otherwise. Owning and controlling the access to information counts more than information per se.

The very 'idea' of information as equivalent to power already masks the process by which some phenomena get upgraded to "information" status while others remain undistinguished. This sorting and storing of info clearly changes the way we know and live. Money becomes information stored in computer banks, rather than cash. A criminal is tied to a crime through DNA rather than by an eyewitness.[22]

Information is not neutral. It defines and is structured by the relations of what Michel Foucault terms power/knowledge.[23] Information appears as disembodied labor and the computer becomes a prosthetic. If information is taken as "fact," as the starting point of power, then access is assumed. There are new layerings of mystification in this scenario, as information displaces its origins. Karl Marx could weigh in here. The modes of information and "mental production" are ALREADY imbricated in the relations of capital.[24]

Capitalists still want labor; they just need less of it and in different form because of digital technologies. Although Nicholas

Negroponte believes that the digital landscape frees us from old prejudices and initiates a "common language" that can foster "greater world harmony," he does not take into account the conflict between workers and corporate power's love affair with digital knowledge.[25]

Information, as a form of disembodied labor, becomes a commodity to buy and sell. Computer literacy then becomes a commercial fashion, not a specific skill. There is always a new program to buy or computer upgrade to consider. Rapid obsolescence defines the products, as well as labor.[26] This quick turnover of computer goods has a real effect on what we are able to know and access. Given the short life span of any data-processing program, archival knowledge might truly become a thing of the past. Within a few years, disks filled with info will be unreadable on new programs.[27]

Already, there are information-rich and information-poor individuals, and this status is tied to one's relation to capital and the 'old' modes of ownership and control in their *new digitized forms.* Nondigitized forms of labor and kinds of knowing have less status in this new info society, but this does not mean that information has moved beyond class privilege.[28] Given the new digital technologies, information has unique autonomous potential in its breadth and speed of distribution, but it does not flow freely from corporate/media-ted moorings.

The move from agriculture, to manufacture, to transportation and energy production, to digitized-info sources is all part of the same narrative.[29] Given that, the computer is not working-class friendly. It displaces the very idea of labor. Computers represent power: "selling computers is about selling power."[30] The machine supposedly replaces the person. With no laborers to be found—only cyber/information—who needs Marx or the former soviet union? No surprise that the first political casualty of the information age was the bureaucratic statist-soviet system. Its model of hierarchical industrial inflexibility did not stand a chance against "world informatization."[31]

Labor is in trouble. Between 1983 and 1993, u.s. banks replaced 37 percent of their workforce with automated teller machines (ATMs). China is planning to introduce computerized production, which is expected to eliminate 20 million jobs.[32] Worldwide unemployment is expected to continue to increase. Already, more than 800 million people are underemployed or entirely without a job.[33] Meanwhile, profits are at an all-time high due to digital technology and jobless recoveries, where profits increase and jobs decrease.

There are new class relations to be understood here. The modes of information are key, but so *also* are the class relations of racial/sexual power that define access to information. Computers displace people and also surveil the laborer. Despite the hype, labor remains crucial, even when disembodied. These new-old relations require reforms of tax and copyright law to assist the process of accumulation for the new winners.

The emergence of a high-tech-info economy requires new tax laws that assist its beneficiaries.[34] The Reagan-Bush decade of the 1980s put much of this new law in place. By 1992, the richest 1 percent of americans gained 91 percent in after-tax income while the poorest fifth lost 17 percent of their income. This has led to the top 1 percent's total income equaling that of 40 percent of the population.[35]

Bill Gates sees the PC as the "foundation for the next revolution." According to Gates, we will be able to access any information we want on the internet. He also warns, however, that we must be careful to "make sure the upcoming highway doesn't become a pirate's paradise." His obvious concern is to rewrite intellectual property rights for the digital world.[36] This rewriting also effectively challenges antitrust legislation.

Gates's Microsoft empire has set up restrictive contracts with its customers, announced software that does not exist, and bullied smaller software companies. In reaction to this activity, the Justice department, in *U.S. v. Microsoft* (1998), denounced Gates for stifling competition and attempting to monopolize access to the net. Because Gates lost this round, he is now busy lobbying more directly in his own behalf.

Law is always called on to assist realignments of power. In this instance, law must fine-tune intellectual property for the digital age. The first attempt to adapt copyright law to the digital realm started, interestingly enough, in 1989, alongside the fall of communism. More recently, the 1995 *Report of the Working Group on Intellectual Property* was initiated by the Clinton administration in order to pave the way for the so-called information highway.

The report examines how new communications technologies increase the ease and speed with which documents are disseminated and therefore necessitate new protective legislation for the creators and owners of intellectual property.[37] Copyright protection is pivotal to this process. Unauthorized use must be clearly delineated, even though copyright's initial intent was "to increase and not to impede the harvest of knowledge."[38]

These concerns with copyright are tied to the issue of marketability: there must be an incentive for free expression, and this incentive is based on protecting authorship. But now ideas can be stored, communicated, and distributed without recognizing authorship. With these new forms of dissemination and transmission, copyright has lost its authority. The Clinton group's report resubstantiates the rights of the copyright holder. The 'owners' are privileged against the users here.[39]

In response, in the fall, 1996 the White House proposed the National Information Infrastructure Copyright Protection Act (NIICPA) in an attempt to once again rewrite property for the net and specifically limit the sharing of commercial software. The act turns the internet into a toll road for the 'owners' even though the 'knowledge brokers' are already doing quite well. Bill Gates was worth more than $18 billion *before* NIICPA.[40]

A comprehensive telecom and information policy will rewrite copyright for the national information infrastructure (NII) and the global information network. The World Intellectual Property Organization (WIPO) gathering in Geneva in 1997 again sought to clarify copyright use, particularly in regard to its fair-use clause—the right to use/reproduce copyrighted works for noncommercial purposes. Hollywood, along with media publishing conglomerates, had become quite dissatisfied with the way libraries, as well as service providers, were disseminating materials they saw as their own.

The u.s. contingent went to the Geneva meetings fully intending to try and make the net safe for Hollywood's and the publishing industry's business interests. But representatives from africa, asia, latin america, and sometimes scandinavia, stood powerfully against this initiative.[41] Hollywood and its allies were unable to have the idea of 'fair use' rewritten to their commercial advantage.

Part and parcel of these legal maneuvers is the cyber-media-corporate scramble for positioning. Once again, 1989 was a significant moment, with the establishment of the World Wide Web and, with it, a new accessibility to the net. By 1995, MCI, ATT, Sprint, and IBM, along with media conglomerates, replaced the government as the net's overseer and major investor. The revolutions of 1989 and their displacement of government regulation are hardly limited to eastern europe. The u.s. government has also been displaced—though inconsistently—by the race toward privatization.

The net traces its origins to the early 1960s, in a Rand Corporation project to establish and maintain national defense in case of nuclear war. The system's purpose was to create a decentralized network that could function in a national emergency. Computers across the country doing defense-related work were hooked up to each other through ARPAnet (for Advanced Research Projects Agency) and formed the infrastructure of the 'information superhighway.'[42] Today, telecom/media companies own the infrastructure, originally built for the military, on which the information society rests.

By 1995, NSFnet (for National Science Foundation) had been replaced by National Research and Education Network (NREW), a series of *private* firms using *public* money to subsidize their interests. In the meantime, the government granted the communications information network the license to rewire the united states. Gore continuously speaks of greater public access while protecting corporate greed.[43] The White House Information Infrastructure Task Force (IITF) defines its agenda as protecting competition, providing a "flexible new regulatory framework," and "encouraging private investment" in the NII.[44]

Private firms, using public monies, dominate policy debates and decisions in the information age. Data, video, and telephone corporations lobby and make campaign contributions on their own behalf. Disney contributed large sums of money to both parties in the 1995–96 election season. And so, the telecom/media industries—transmission providers, online service providers, software manufacturers, film and t.v. studios, and publishers—stake out their claims.[45] Once again, Disney, News-Corp, General Electric, Universal, Sony, Microsoft, and Time Warner merge in new partnerships. Microsoft, that monopolistic leviathan of computer software companies, now owns 11.5 percent interest in Comcast, the fourth-largest u.s. cable television operator, ensuring a new consolidation of cyber-media power.[46]

The NII will cost half a *trillion* dollars to build over the next twenty years. The same government that has rewritten social welfare law and ended 'hand-outs' to the poor has in 1997 *given away* digital spectrum worth up to $70 billion to commercial broadcasters. The largest media companies in the world got the equivalent of at least five new channels in every market where they currently own one.[47]

New ways to communicate, distribute, *and* control information are springing up all the time. Decentralized information networks run on top of and through new-old hierarchies of privilege. The internet "is not a new form of life . . . just a new activity," according to Esther Dyson.[48] As such, it supplies creative possibilities for inclusivity *and* exclusivity.

Although a new cyberlanguage has evolved—netoyens, netizens, netiquette—it is not self-evident that these cyberarenas are communities unto themselves. Much of life on the net mirrors the imaginings of 'real-life' nations and families and is, as such, an idealized fantasy. AOL, says Elizabeth Lewis in *WIRED*, is a family like the Reagans were.[49] Neither AOL nor the Reagans, according to their daughter Patty, know how to 'really' nurture and care for their own. In 1996, after a huge promotion promising unlimited monthly access for $19.95, tons of AOL users couldn't even get online. Thousands quit the service, myself included, and others decided to sue.

Family, nation, *and* cyberspace are complicit here. They each express imaginary fantasies about knowledge and power. Cybertechnologies, along with their protective layerings of 'information discourse,' promote virtual community as the 'real.' But this reality is narrow to begin with and should not be viewed as a universal fact. Kali Tal notes that the 'we' of the net is the white, upper-class, male self.[50] Majorities of people all over the world are left out while virtual reality *permits* escape. Real-world devastation can be ignored because it is not in view.

This, however, is not the whole story. Whereas one may use cyberlife to escape, another may use it for wholly different purposes. There are new technological capacities for truly interactive democratic communication and participatory deliberation even though these capacities stand in stark contrast to the privatization and commercialization of information itself. This is why the Institute for Global Communications (IGC), the u.s. member of the Association for Progressive Communications (APC), seeks to refocus the net toward the progressive information needs of all people. But what is it about technology *per se* that allows for the progressive possibility of un-doing power systems IF that is how people direct it?

CyberReal/CyberVirtual

Virtual reality can shove aside reality, limited as it is by the constraints of body and place. It can also take one closer to reality, like a simulated molecule can enable one to see reality more clearly. Or one might say, similar to Paul Virilio, that reality is pluralized or split into two forms, one actual, the other virtual.[51] Virtual reality thus expresses an epistemology about information, about what and how we know, as much as (or maybe more than) it is a mechanized spatial location or geography about computers. Cyberlanguage, then, expresses a politics of body and mind, labor and technology.

In this scenario, cyberspace is not simply "an imaginary space that exists entirely inside a computer."[52] Cyberculture derives from the relations that develop with and from the information housed in the computer. The boundaries of the computer are not quite clear because it embodies relations that exist both inside and outside the machine itself, connecting the user and the computer. The computer becomes in this instance a prosthesis—an extension of the physical body.[53] As an extension, the body is not amputated, as Marshall McLuhan assumed, nor is the body simply 'dead meat,' a mere container for the brain, as some cybergeeks would have it.[54]

Virtual reality becomes a means of externalization.[55] The hybrid status of person and machine negates the computer as a box, or the autonomy of information/technology. Technology meshes with the people and the information/labor who make it and use it. Alternative worlds, synthetic images and sounds, allow us to think/dream/fantasize in new and different ways. According to Vilem Flusser, new worlds can "emerge from the computer" as "digital apparitions" let us "know that we dream." Possibilities can be realized at our computers.[56]

Michael Benedikt sees cyberspace as a "parallel universe created and sustained by the world's computers and communication lines." It is an electronic space, networked globally, generating an artifical, 'virtual' reality.[57] In this sense, virtual does not simply mean leaving 'the' body behind. Instead, something new is created. There is a threading beyond real and unreal, ideal and true. Cybertech and bodies fuse and pluralize each other. But there is no inevitable set of outcomes.

For Donna Haraway, silicon breast implants, plastic/cosmetic surgery, and Agent Orange are examples of fusing bodies and technology in ways that are not liberatory.[58] Computer technologies can be used to rebuild a body, or create a new mask for it. It has gotten to the point where the 'ideal' woman's body is no longer 'real'—it is imaged on a computer. A waist can be pinched, breasts lifted, cheekbones made more prominent, all with a few taps of the mouse. Perfection is no longer human, it is virtual.[59] There are nonhuman, posthuman perfections that are no longer limited to real bodies. With no end to imagined perfection, there is likewise no end to the oppressiveness of perfection.[60]

Technology already em*bodies* the hybrid power/effect of body/machine. Haraway writes of athletes as "high performance machines."[61] The culture is high-tech and machines realign the territory of the body. So bodies are rebuilt, or maybe abandoned as one enters a computer screen. Leaving the body behind is neither simply real nor virtual because cyberspaces are habitats of the imagination.[62] The real sparks imaginings; lived experience enters the virtual.[63] Then the virtual is in part real, the real in part virtual. This unique relationship can thrive in computer-mediated spaces because of the increased capacity for anonymous freedom.

Computer-based technologies allow for an "extension of the human imagination."[64] They defy the constraining boundaries of the physical world and initiate the "infinity of imagination."[65] Susie Bright argues that 'fantasy' itself is the ultimate virtual experience and that she prefers to take her body with her, rather than lose it. She is not looking for an "out of body experience" but rather new experiences with her body.[66]

All this said, it is precisely the boundaries of lived experience that also, inevitably, initiate imagination. The relations of mind, body, and machine are not wholly cybernew AND there is something unique to having these relations digitally wired. After all, George Eliot left her body behind and gave it a man's name long before cyberanonymity.[67] WIRING transcends the "sensorial and organic architecture of the human body"[68] and creates new transnational cyberspaces.

Fluctuating and changing boundaries can intoxicate. The real somehow does not seem enough anymore; yet, simultaneously, reality becomes too much.[69] Living on the net allows an alternate life. As one user says: "We are more equal on the net because we can either ignore or create the body that appears in cyberspace."[70] Trying to free oneself from the restrictions of the body is by definition a neverending process. But freedom from the body is a temporary/virtual status. The 'real' body continues with its demands.

A lot can happen in cyberlife. People fall in love by e-mail. One woman says she fell in love but it happened in her substitute body, online, while she stayed up later and was more playful.[71] Journalist Meghan Daum says her affair on the net was "more authentic than much of what she experienced in the daylight." She found the process was both fascinating and repelling. She writes: "All the tangible stuff fell away. My body did not exist. I had no skin, no hair, no bones. All desire had converted itself into a cerebral current that reached nothing but my frontal lobe." There was no outdoors, no weather, just the screen and the phone and the chair. Then all came crashing down when they met. The romance was quickly over.[72]

Some networks, such as WELL (Whole Earth 'Lectronic Link), bring a gift of extended family to some, a "disembodied tribe" to others.[73] One user says she had her first family dinners on the net.[74] These new communities are real though virtual. Both RL (real life) and VR (virtual reality) are REAL because local circumstance structures border crossings and because body, mind, and machine remain semi-autonomous and webbed.[75]

New terrain is created by transnational telecommunications technologies that connect people across geographical divides.[76] Experience is stretched, enhanced, and fabricated. The local/global and individual/community dissemble to create new postnational imaginaries.[77] What emerges are seamless and new "ways of being fictive" when fictive can also mean real.[78] These new social locations are marked and different albeit decentered from one's "off-line life."[79]

Hackers take full advantage of the potentially democratic uses of cybertechnologies. They are touted by some as the true democrats on the net. They believe one should be able to access anything, anywhere.[80] They take Bill Gates at his word when he says that "we are all created equal in the virtual world" even if "virtual-equity" is much easier to achieve than "real-world equity."[81]

Virtual equity may be quite different from "real-world equity," but cybertechnologies can still enable prodemocracy struggles in Chiapas, mexico; Beijing, china; and Belgrade, serbia. Faxes and e-mails, subverting authoritarian regimes, have carried messages of these struggles to the rest of the world.[82]

Democracy, Sex, and Cyberspaces

If computers, like most forms of technology, act as prostheses for the body, they do so within the problematic racialized and sexualized meanings of our bodies. 'The' body is 'reality' in the flesh. Bodies speak sex/gender/race in the flesh. Computers realign and refashion these fascinations and obsessions. The censorship of porn as a panacea solution for controlling sex on the net misrepresents, oversimplifies, and misunderstands sex and the racializing of gender in cyberrelations.[83]

If gender can be morphed any which way, infinite new possibilities arise to experience sexual freedom as well as sexual/racial exploitation in cyberspace. The possibilities of sexual and gender fantasy—both virtual and real—are boundless. This means that cyberspace has the capacity to both liberate and oppress women of all colors in new-old real/virtual ways.

Then again, in the age of AIDS and other sexual diseases, text sex is safe sex. "There is a certain kind of freedom in virtual sex," writes Mark Dery. No fluids. No bodies. Just a screen where one writes: "ImmmmmmCommmmmmingggg."[84] In virtual reality "you are whoever you say you are." Or, you think you are whoever you pretend to be. You experience the erotic without having to actually share your body.[85] Cyberculture dreams of machine sex, and sex machines unleash new imaginaries and fantasies.

Not all cyberians adopt this techno/sexual stance. They argue that the fantasies are still of the body, or bodies. Even if desire can be displaced onto machines, bodies remain in the desire.[86] As R. U. Sirius says: "sex is the only good excuse for emobodiment."[87] His fantasy is to free the body and extend the possibilities of real bodies. He is not sure what "cyberbodies" REALLY, honestly, are.

Affairs on the net are both salient and 'only' cyber. Virtual infidelity is 'just talk' and it is also real. Some monogamous partners allow their lovers to have e-mail affairs, which are seen as different than real/body encounters. A shared mind is different than a shared body. Others do not accept this rationale. For some, virtual infidelity expresses real desire, a response to real loneliness, a real longing for connectedness and intimacy. So is virtual reality less real than a reality defined by flesh?

The border/boundaries of mind and body continue to frame the tensions between real/virtual, labor/digital, and power/information. The body remains at issue here: technology's struggle to control, extend, and extract from it. Sometimes the struggle is over labor, sometimes it is over sex and its gendered/racialized meaning, and sometimes it is both. AND, this structures the struggle over power in the info/tech society.

Consider the provocative potential of being wired by erotic desires. Abandon the body and there are promises of heightened sexual satisfaction: cerebral sex replaces bodily contact, although stereotypical gender often remains. Claudia Springer says that technology is fully eroticized in this cyborg—part human/part machine—stance. Even though technology has no sex, the "representations of technology often do." But this relation is ambiguous because computers present an "asexual surface" on which to write.[88]

Sexual opportunities expand, anonymous experimentation seems easy, and curiosity is piqued. The subversive potential of the net, where sex and freedom can meet, undermines the hierarchy of patriarchal families and censorious civil society. Sex and gender order the power-effect of culture as a whole. When gender boundaries defining masculinity and femininity begin to loosen, even in virtual spaces, they unsettle patriarchal heterosexual traditions. Censoring porn legitimizes the gatekeeping of gender and textsex. AND, as importantly, it authorizes the discipline and control of 'the' body in ways not confined to sex per se.

Some men gender-bend on the net, saying they are women, not in order to hook a woman, but rather to interact with women in a new way. They say they like the intimacy between women, an intimacy to which they do not have access as men. Posing as a woman allows for "an ecstatic dream of disembodiment."[89] One could also just say this is a new-old form of voyeurism.

Even with the swapping and pretense, however, standard gender expectations often continue.[90] Traditional notions of masculinity and femininity continue through the disembodiment. Even in a Grrrlove Mailing List we find mention of cunts, and bitches, and assbands.[91]

Anything supposedly goes: from flirtation to cross-dressing to 'virtual rape.'[92] But some net users think 'net-rape' crosses the line of the acceptable. The ensuing debate centers on whether 'net-rape' is real or whether it is, to enlist Catharine MacKinnon's phrase, "only words." Rape assaults the body; 'net-rape' assaults the mind. Rape, through words on a screen, is described, not acted. Yet, violence toward girls and women on the screen can seem "all too real," as either "fantasies being explored" or "past deeds being recounted."[93]

The net has more than its share of real-world ugliness. Nasty words and images are sent over the wires in the form of 'flame wars.' And cybergirls and women are in the minority. Only 15 percent of *WIRED* magazine authors are women.[94] Less than 10 percent of public messages are posted by women even though 30 percent of internet-access accounts belong to women.[95] Hackers are predominantly men[96] and the internet remains as male as the Wild Wild West.[97]

These masculinist moorings limit netfreedom for women and girls. So the net extends more (sexual) freedom to men, much like the 'real' world. Middle- and upper-class white men have more freedom because of their privileged status. Racial and sexual equality does not exist on the net, and this unequal footing defines netfreedom. Lots of verbal intimidation and harassment occur as a result.[98]

Yet, some white women and people of color will pretend to be (white) men on the net and enjoy more freedom as such. They can present themselves as aloof and not be seen as weird because as white men they are allowed this distant stance, whereas women are expected to be available and open. One woman programmer reveals the promise she feels: "Get online and have completely equal footing with men around the world." She unknowingly exposes the parameters of netgender when she says: "As a female, I was a man among men."[99]

Amidst all this, censoring porn seems a bit beside the point—or is it? Censorship of the net is justified, some claim, to protect women and children. This discourse of paternalist protectionism reifies old gender borders. In response, Donna Riley asks, Why aren't women better protected from real violence?[100] Why aren't real girls encouraged to visit cyberspace? Make cyberspace and the real world girl-friendly. Develop more "friendship adventures for girls" rather than "lone commandos" or "Barbie Fashion Designer CD-Roms."[101] End the sexual abuse and economic exploitation of children.

Even though the net reproduces old forms of sexual and racial privilege more than it unsettles them, cybertechnologies ALSO contain a radical potential for the undoing of racialized and sexualized identities. Because of this, it should be no surprise to see more attempts at controlling internet use around the globe. In iran, as in the united states, the concern is to create access to good morals; "a certain level of decency must be provided." This statist/moralist stance connotes the interrelationship between sexual/cultural borders AND global capital. Whereas global capital and its cyber-media complex attempt to erase economic borders, sexual and racialized boundary lines are another story.

But what if the desire for democracy is as much about sexual choices as it is about economic subsistence? Then the politics to control the net and access to its 'information' is a struggle over the meaning of democracy. One adamant internet user in iran loves the new cultural freedom and says he will stay online no matter what. He muses: "What's the worst they can do, execute me?"[102] This is a problematic choice at best: cyberdemocracy or 'real' death.

Virtual Democracy and Cyberfreedom

Power relations structure the real/virtual divide. "Freedom comes out of the wire of a modem,"[103] and this freedom is not equally distributed. Yet, digital technology has the potential to undermine existing relations of power. The flow of information cannot be contained. The internet creates new lines of communication and challenges older constructions of private/public dialogue.

This remains of great concern to governments across the globe. Pakistan and iran limit net availability; china rejects "absolute freedom of information"; many middle east nations control political and religious discussion; vietnam and saudi arabia control internet service through a single government-controlled gateway; exorbitant rates are charged for net use in india; and the Clinton administration supported the Communications Decency Act.[104]

In an 'information' society the tension between equality and freedom can be seen with new clarity. The info society and its cybertech promise of freedom embrace an individualism premised on privatization and consumerism. In contrast, equality—in terms of economic class, sexual orientation, and gender and/or racial fairness—challenges hierarchical relations based on these schemata. Equality remains potentially subversive as a 'really' democratic discourse demanding access to labor, information, and technology. Equality discourse challenges the media/corporate control of cybertechnology.

Cyberdiscourse applauds the neoliberal commitment to freedom: of the market, of the superhighway, of information routes themselves. But individual freedom must reckon with the structured limitations of actualizing freedom. As I have said before, one may have the *freedom* to receive electronic information, but one must have *equality* to do so: a computer, the software, the training, and a telephone line. One may have the freedom to electronically communicate with anyone across the globe, but one must first secure an e-mail address.

The more public funds are cut—for schools, libraries, and the computers for them—the less access exists for those without individual equipment. Spending on local libraries fell to about $100 million in 1996, compared to several billion dollars for prison construction.[105] The problem is one of public access for individuals without private means. There is a harmful cycle already in place. The less access, the less equality. The less the equality, the less access. This is why public access to information and the skills needed for finding, understanding, and using it is so critical.[106] Freedom, however, remains a proposition of self-sufficiency.

Global telecommunications networks are not the originators of the tension between individual freedom and access within the social/political/economic structure. But new layers of technological elitism have been created, along with new forms of obfuscation to justify the inequality.

The wealthy white males of cyberculture applaud its non-hierarchical interactions. They celebrate the cyberarenas where authorities and experts have no special status. Not surprisingly, some women choose to differ with this assessment. These cyberwomen think "technology serves as a site for the reinscription of cultural narratives of gendered and racial identities."[107] Men like the net because they can escape (real) women there. The net reminds men of the good old days of 'men only' clubs. Gender hierarchy seems completely democratic to men, to whom it is transparent, because the rules operate in their favor.

Masculinism exists on the net and in cyberrelations because masculinist relations are already in part embodied in their technological designs and interactional methods. Technology is embedded in the engendered meanings and structures of science itself. These masculinist underpinnings digitize sexism in newly abstract form. The digital coding, which is determined by a binary system which is an oppositional rather than a relational dialogic system, structurally reencodes the masculine/feminine divide. The format of communication is linear and singular. This kind of prosthetic communication allows the real body—with its physicality of racialized sexuality—to appear in the form of digitized info.[108] Digitizing gender—in numerical neutral codes—amplifies sexism with new formats of racial apartheid. High-tech obfuscates these systems of power.

The 'real' demands that we look at the problem of equality. But the net is concerned, instead, with freedom. And freedom gets defined as unfettered speech. So instead of discussing equal access, or freedom of sexual/gender choice, a debate forms about porn.

In June 199, a three-judge federal panel ruled unanimously that the government's attempts to halt the exposure of indecent material on the internet were unconstitutionally broad. The panel rejected the proposed Communications Decency Act (CDA) because the act limited liberty, which is dependant on "the chaos and cacophony of the unfettered speech the 1st amendment protects."[109] The judges applauded the net as the "most participatory marketplace of mass speech that this country—and indeed the world—has yet seen."[110]

In June 1997, the Supreme Court declared the CDA unconstitutional. Speech on the internet was extended the highest level of First Amendment protection. Justice John Paul Stevens, writing for the Court, states: "We have repeatedly recognized the governmental interest in protecting children from harmful materials. But that interest does not justify an unnecessarily broad suppression of speech addressed to adults."[111] Freedom of speech wins the day along with consumer marketing.

The participatory marketplace, as we have seen, is also an exclusive club. But cyberdialogue is self-referential: once you are inside, it is easy to forget that many are left out. It is also not clear that the marketplace of mass speech is always interactive or participatory. Afterall, much information is simply received, but not discussed and evaluated. The format of cyberdialogue can be incredibly passive. The parameters of discussion are rule-bound. The technologies themselves require a predetermined format of exploration. One arrows forward or backward, up or down, signals yes or no. There is no code for maybe.

Newt Gingrich's imaginary electronic republic assumes us each rich in information access. (Let them eat computers?) Government has no role to play other than to leave the information society to the machinations of the cyber-media-corpo-rate complex and full-scale commercialism.[112]

Digital computer technology is producing "high tech data pushers" who are in the business of selling personal informa-tion for marketing purposes.[113] For much on the net, one needs to keep a credit card close at hand. Some e-mail providers trade free service to their subscribers for advertiser's rights to send them info. Unauthorized commercialism poses even more of a threat to subscribers.

Many of the most useful attributes of information are un-dermined by this commercialization.[114] There is no mention of collecting information in some kind of electronic world archive or Library of Congress. Only that which is profitable is deemed worthwhile.[115] Information and its storage are not neutral processes.

Instead of information access—for students, researchers, or scientists—profits set the priorities of the internet. The pack-aging and sorting of information by companies like AOL or Netscape narrow the information database. During the 1996 presidential election AT&T built "Ballot Net," a form of high-tech campaigning that distributed automated election infor-mation. It built the network for free as a political contribution to the Clinton campaign.[116] This does not bode well for an in-formation-rich deliberative democracy: a town square built by AT&T.

The cyber-media-corporate complex is firmly in place for the twenty-first century. More than $20 million in campaign contributions over the past decade have come from the telecommunications industries. The local telephone industry has given $17.3 million to political action committees in the decade since the breakup of AT&T.[117] This complex supplies the mandarins of the electronic kingdom. They promise a technotopia and hype the data superhighway. They applaud the inevitability of digital reality. The result is a world divided into privileged virtual economies, passive storage depots for cheap labor and permanently enslaved nations like haiti.[118] In the end, cyberculture perpetuates and normalizes massive unemployment by justifying a hostile relationship among people, their labor, and high-tech machines.

Almost two-thirds of u.s. homes have cable service, about 94 percent have telephones, and 98 percent have color televisions. Almost as many have VCRs. These percentages highlight large differences between the united states and poor countries around the world AND reveal huge new markets for cybergoods still to be captured by the cyber-media-corporate complex.

The imbalance of wealth and telecom accessibility has a devastating effect on countries of the third and fourth worlds. With almost half of the world's population having never made a telephone call, and more than 70 percent of africa's population living in villages with no electricity, the problem of global communications equality becomes critically important. The Global MacBride Round Table was founded—interestingly again in 1989—to advance the 'right' to world information and communication as a fundamental democratic right for all people.[119]

Democratic communication becomes more than freedom of speech—it requires access. The demand for access challenges the First Amendment right to free speech in new and meaningful ways. The new technologies and cyberdiscourses exacerbate the limitations of freedom to communicate when one does not have the ability to do so.

Guillermo Gómez-Peña imagines a democratized cyberspace. He asks to "brownify virtual space; to 'spanglishize' the net; to 'infect' the lingua franca; to exchange a different sort of information—mythical, poetical, political, performative, imagistic; and . . . to find grassroots applications to new technologies."[120] He wants to help Latino youth exchange their guns for computers and to link community centers around the country on the net.

The Centre for Communication and Human Rights, with participants from the netherlands, the Third World Network and other progressive groups, has published "The People's Communication Charter" (PCC). The PCC demands equitable access to local and global communication resources and facilities and a diversity of languages because communication is basic to the life of all individuals.[121] Much like the Global MacBride Round Table, the PCC seeks recognition of communication as a human right, as a way of building a global movement that focuses on the quality of public communication and information. At the New Delhi Symposium on New Technologies and the Democratization of Audiovisual Communication in 1994, the participants agreed that airwaves and satellite paths are a "global people's resource" and should be shared equitably. Participatory democracy should be the goal of these information technologies.[122]

In order to democratize cyberspace—as both a location and an epistemology—one must unmask its relations of power. To democratize information, we must address the inequalities that structure cyberspaces and define the technologies of cyberspace; the inequalities that control access to these realms; the inequalities of the 'right' to communicate; and the inequalities resulting from the privatization of public spaces. Otherwise, cyberspace will remain a virtual reality for the few.

Social and economic justice must replace advertising and profits. Reciprocity and deliberation must replace passivity. Benefits and largesse must be distributed among the many and not monopolized by a few. People must be more important than digits and bits of data.[123]

It is not easy to imagine a public life rich in deliberative democratic processes. But, strangely, it is possible to do so because the very technologies that are premised in real-world exploitation also create a cyberassisted subversive viewing of these new excesses of global capital. The contradiction between the exploitative uses of these new cybertechnologies and their use for a liberatory politics allows for a new, even if skeptical, sense of hope.

4
surviving

Transnations, Global Capital, and Families

surviving

Now I want to view the globe not only as a media-ted imaginary space of cyberrealism, but as an arena of transnational capitalist exploitation and environmental degradation. This is no easy task because the cyber-media lens through which we inevitably view the world structures our perception of it. Capital accumulation is neutralized by endless advertising that censors imaginings critical of consumer culture.

The very same information systems that connect parts of the globe also obscure the relations of power I wish to expose. On the one hand, the internet advertises universal connectivity. On the other hand, Paul Virilio sees this entire project as disabling—all we have done is to shrink an already polluted globe.[1]

U.S. airline tickets are processed in barbados, jamaica, haiti, india, china, and other countries,[2] while documented workers still need passports to move from one country to another. In the first instance, there are no economic borders. In the second instance, the political nation, as such, is retained. Nation AND globe hold significance, but in a new and chaotic way.

Coca-Cola describes itself not as a multinational corporation, but as multi/local. The local becomes globalized and the global localized. In this process of global localization, borders are crossing and markets are segmented to increase flexible production.[3] Local and global, though no longer separate, remain significant. Virilio takes a slightly different view, arguing that the global has delocalized the local, creating "glocalization." The disaster at Chernobyl is his proof: Radioactive fallout recognizes no local borders.[4]

Electronic media grant consumer culture new capabilities to construct 'the' globe. Consumption becomes a central facet of work itself, or as Arjun Appadurai terms it: consumption becomes the process of "disciplining the imagination."[5] At issue is the cultural production of a transnational imaginary that views the globe as unified. Consumer culture both tunnels and disciplines our vision. The imagination becomes conformist and universal. Local sites then often try to remain 'different', as a form of resistance.[6] Such resistance is hard to sustain, but it happens nevertheless with the Zapatistas in Chiapas, mexico, antiwar feminist activists in Belgrade, and environmental grassroots movements throughout africa.

Imagination, however, can never be completely controlled. So the globe also becomes undisciplined via the very same cyber-media system that protects capital.[7] Telecommunications networks connect people to promissory visions from which they also feel excluded. Even if one is privileged enough to have a foreign currency credit card in china, 'foreign' goods are often too expensive to buy.

Yet, the globe can also be oppositionally 'imagined' as a potentially REAL community. Then the habitability of the world, rather than consumer possibilities, defines the agenda. Then demands for environmental sanity and public health become the focus for a majority of people yearning for a better life across the globe.

While high-tech goes global, economic class divisions—often expressed racially and sexually—are reconstituted across and in geographical nations. Women and girls of color become/remain the poorest of the poor across the globe. This racialized patriarchy is as universal as capitalism itself.

Universal does not mean homogeneous or singular.[8] Capital defines itself in plural forms through the racial and gender structuring of different cultures. Families and nations are renegotiated in the process: capitalism, nationalism, and racialized patriarchy displace and replace each other as public and private terrains are exploited by consumer capitalism.

Transnational corporations restructure nation-states; the traditional patriarchal nuclear family, no matter how un-'real,' remains a constant imaginary; a few women enter management and government office, to little avail; and racialized patriarchy is reconstituted along with the nation-state for global capital. I will explore these processes in order to reveal the power nexus of the global information age. Fissures and rumblings from these sites just might instigate a challenge to the dominance of global capital and its cyber-media complex.

On States, Nations, and Families

Economic nations are increasingly displaced by twenty-first-century transnational corporations. This is not to say that the nation-state is in demise, but rather that it is being re-formed for twenty-first-century global capitalist racialized patriarchy. This redefinition narrows the public responsibility of the nation-state. In this newly privatized nation-state, social welfare and other government functions are relocated to alternate sites such as family, church, and private volunteer groups. The imaginary globe replaces the imagined economic nation while the political nation gets privatized.[9]

Meanwhile, capital, which has new global capacity, underpins the contradictory status of globalism for laborers, rather than capitalists. Clearly, capital roams more freely than labor. Or, as Aijaz Ahmad threatens: "Let all the U.S. capital come to India and all the Indian workers go to the U.S. to earn U.S. wages."[10]

Nations are defined by very different economic realities from within. As economic inequality in the united states increases, people are forced to live amid but also within and across the divisions of several economies. Heightened inequities and excess exist side by side. Since World War II the chasm between rich and poor has never been greater.[11] Homeless panhandlers beg on the streets in every major u.s. city as part of this new poverty, while new laws are passed to try to stop them. The singularity of corporate power overrides established forms of family and nation. Environmental well-being is in total jeopardy.

This should be terribly unsettling to anyone who must earn a living. Economic nations become pluralized to multiple standards within one geographical area. First and third world no longer simply refer to territorial maps. New York City and Los Angeles provide undocumented apparel workers. Cities in vietnam, indonesia, taiwan, and thailand provide young factory girls for the transnationalized marketplace.

This paints a racialized and gendered division of labor onto the globe.

The past two decades have seen an enormous increase in economic, gender, and racial inequality, as well as degradation of the environment, with women of color living in the most polluted environments.[12] The pollution of water, the depletion of natural resources, the contamination of soil and air falls most harshly upon the world's women as they plant, farm, and build their economies from the land up.

Contrast this to the world of McDonald's, Disney, and Nike that dominates the airwaves. Ben Barber depicts this arena as a universalized culture of videology, infotainment, and Hollyworld.[13] This virtual screen covers over the many economic class realities of people's lives while also creating the consumer desires that enable exploitation.

Consumerism makes the globe seem like one big shopping mall, even for those with little money to participate. Laptops, modems, and fax machines allow millions of people in the united states to telecommute and do their work anywhere.[14] No office space is needed for these workers, just as no one country is needed to house the company. Space, distance, and time are restructured alongside family, nation, and political life.[15]

Global corporations service customers, not citizens.[16] According to Armand Mattellart, corporate expansionism requires new and different political and cultural forms to "continue the accumulation process." The principal target to destroy is the "nation-state and all of its institutional apparatuses," which operate in relation to the nation, rather than the globe. Therefore, the culture industries seek to colonize the state with commercial norms.[17]

Because global capital turns the nation-state into yet another domain of privatized, consumerist activity, the early twenty-first-century will be a strategic moment of enormous importance in the history of bourgeois democratic societies. The state is no longer envisioned as simply harmonizing nation-based interclass conflict, but rather as assisting the mobility of global capital.

The promissory of the nation's public responsibility for its 'tired and poor' has been scrapped. Consumer culture and its industries hold the globe hostage to their own transnational markets. Freedom is positioned against equality and opportunity becomes privatized. Democracy, in the information age, is for those rich enough to access it on their own.

In this scenario, the social welfare nation-state inhibits rather than enables transnational capital.[18] This discourse was successfully institutionalized by neoconservatives in the united states through the 1980s with great effect.[19] Voters, increasingly dissatisfied with 'big government,' became disillusioned and disenfranchised. Barely half of those eligible now vote. Only about 38 percent of eligible u.s. voters went to the polls in 1994, which served the right wing well.

Newt Gingrich mobilized these antigovernment forces for his "Contract with America," which proposed cutting Medicaid, nutrition programs, student loans, environmental protections, and other government programs.[20] Welfare "as we know it" was to end.[21] State support for families with children in need was to be dismantled and replaced by a highly privatized notion of individualism.[22] Less than 20 percent of the vote was needed to endorse this effort.[23] By 1996 Clinton had fully endorsed this view.

In all this posturing, mainstream politics shifts. Media-ted politics begins to look like parody; full of bluster, deceit, and incompetence. On the one hand, electoral politics symbolizes ineffectuality; on the other hand, it continues to fantasize democracy at work. About half of the public pretends and participates; the other half washes its hands of the mess.

John Kennedy, Jr.'s response to these developments is to edit a magazine, *George*, to help people become "skeptical consumers" of politics. Politics, for him, reaches "extravagantly— from elected office to media moguls to movie stars to ordinary citizens." He wants to make images as compelling as prose and to renew the accessibility of political life by making it entertaining.[24] But this sounds a bit too much like Disney's strategy. Consumer culture displaces deliberative politics, which is not simply the same as entertainment, and which often may not be fun.

Global Capital and Racialized Patriarchy

Capital, being transient and fluid, needs the nation-state to embrace new transnational trade agreements and policies. "The meaningful divide is not geography—it is class."[25] And the first-world formula utilizes established racialized/patriarchal relations, once effectively located in the western traditional nuclear family and the social welfare state, but now constructed in transnationalized consumerist and multicultural fashion. The new relationships between global capital and privatized states thread corporate excess through the processes of downsizing, structural adjustment, and new formulations of racialized patriarchy.

Said another way, global capital emasculates first-world nation-states as protectors of the economic nation and refocuses them to its economic transnation status. The nation-state is thus a major player in the process of globalizing capital while giving new license to its racial/sexual formation. The nation-state must now nurture the cyber-media complex of transnational capital, while also appearing to meet the needs of its national constituencies. Government officials are caught between a 'rock and a hard place' today. No wonder presidents look so inept.

In this process, aspects of statist patriarchy—the privileging of men in and through the political/public sphere in distinction from the private sphere of womanhood in the home/family/domestic sphere—are transferred to the transnational gendered division of labor in the information age.[26] Women's exploitation is rewired at computer terminals throughout countries of the south while using more differentiated and varied sites in the north.

Women's/girls' secondary status defines their particularly proletarian role across the globe. But now the privatized nation-state plays a more circuitous role in enforcing this gendered hierarchy. The location of power has been dispersed to multiple sites in the transnational economy, and to the single-parent family headed by women. The first-world nation-state regulates less paternalistically in its diminished social welfare role. Instead, privatized sites like the single-parent family and the market itself economically discipline women/girls.

Global patriarchy is sustained less directly through the privatized nation-state than through the numbing inequalities of the market. As a result, public responsibility has diminished and public life has been privatized. Meanwhile 'the' private sphere of family and personal life has been publicized by endless sex scandal, talk-show confessionals, and exposure of domestic violence. Public/private boundaries appear fluid as the personal has been politicized and politics has been personalized. Patriarchal privilege, like capital itself, is flexible and mobile.

As the partial autonomy of first-world economic nations declines in relation to global capital,[27] the public/private divide no longer substantiates patriarchal privilege as it once did. The newly repositioned economic nation defers to the globe's new boundaries, which unsettle and undermine the traditionally patriarchal familial/public divide. So a few upper-middle-class women fill managerial and government jobs—which have less power than they once did. They manage the public household while men remain the CEOs at the top of the cyber-media transnational complex.

The town in which I live for the first time has a woman superintendent of the local schools, even though the public schools have always been a big employer of women at the lower ranks. The college I teach at has its first woman president, acting provost, and sports director. Janet Reno is the first woman attorney general in u.s. history. Is this a sea change for women OR a redefinition of the locations of patriarchal power—to other sites—during the restructuring of transnational capital?

Transnational capital displaces more and more professional labor in favor of service labor. As educational institutions are downsized and their government subsidies erode, the jobs in these arenas become less desirable and more service oriented. In the process of privatizing the economic nation and restructuring its educational system, more women are allowed entry to manage these denuded and downsized arenas of power. It is not that these arenas are no longer important, but rather that they are defined for a different role by global capital and its consumerist culture.

As transnational corporations have gained the upper hand in the power struggle with western governments, 'the' family once again, as in the 1950s, becomes a fantasmatic haven. With the social welfare state in tatters, 'the' family is further displaced from its previous moorings by a dysfunctional government. Traditional family units crumble under the strain while patriarchal male privilege establishes new locations. Increasing numbers of middle-class and poor women fend for themselves and their children.

Meanwhile, preoccupation with 'the' family crisscrosses every kind of politics. Louis Farrakhan organized the Million Man March to proclaim Black men's return to their families as head of the household. Dan Quayle is resurrecting his profamily campaign for the next presidential election. Hundreds of thousands of African-American women took to the streets of Philadelphia in 1997 to use the power of their numbers to "help solidify family relationships and solve the ills that plague their communities."[28] The complicated life history of Black families reflects the racist moorings of nation-state family policy. It is in this context that many Black women struggle to retain autonomy and promote familial responsibility.

Francis Fukuyama, also giving voice to a familial politics argues that families are a source of "social capital" and "rich associational life." Family lessens the need for state power.[29] However, the crises facing family life today in part reflect weakened government support instigated by corporate downsizing. Families have suffered right along with the workers who inhabit them as people have lost jobs or had their jobs redefined, or lost governmental supports such as food stamps and supplemental income.

Dysfunctional families highlight the reckless abandon of transnational capital and its privatized nation-state form. Families cannot fully absorb the responsibilities that were once addressed in part by government agencies. No wonder there is so much fantasmatic 'talk' of family from varied quarters.

While nation, globe, and home are renegotiated for transnational capital, earlier forms of state and familial patriarchal privilege are relocated to the economic class divisions among women and between men and women. Many domestic and familial responsibilities are transplanted to the market itself. So McDonald's and Pizza Hut do their own sort of family cooking, but for profit.

Patriarchal privilege relocates itself in new formulations of the public/private, nation/family divide. This means that masculinist privilege operates through a series of signs that are actually disconnected from their earlier forms and points of origin. The traditional patriarchal family still operates in hyperreal fashion, defining other 'real' family forms as deviant. The new forms of patriarchal privilege written into transnational globalism are tied both to traditional 'signs' of femaleness and to new media-ted fantasies of privatized government.

Women are still considered the second sex as they reproduce the world. Our reproductive bodies are still key in these negotiations for the twenty-first century. This is why the uncertainty about abortion and the need to control women's bodies remains constant within the otherwise changing dynamics of twenty-first century masculinism.

Sex scandal—from the stories told by Gennifer Flowers, Paula Jones, Monica Lewinsky, and Kathleen Willey about their sexual encounters with President Clinton to the sex harassment and adultery charges in the military—loosen the parameters of the public/private, political/personal, and family/nation divides. U.S. politics has no monopoly here: sex scandal rocks japan, france, argentina, and england alike. One can almost see the reconstitution of the state through a kind of gender reconstruction. Constructs of masculinist hierarchy and privilege— within government and military realms—appear flawed and overexposed. And yet in the aftermath of all the sexual charges, sexual harassment as an estimable offense for women in the workplace will be greatly narrowed and lessened in its effect. Of course, the u.s. presidency has been overexposed in all this as well. But Clinton will remain in office, much like Officer Gene McKinney, who escaped punishment for allegedly harassing six military women, while women in the workplace will have lost serious political ground.

I do not mean to *over*globalize the power of capital, or its relation to patriarchy. Nor do I mean to universalize one twenty-first-century nation-state form. Important regional and national differences remain. Japanese capital is both transnational and aggressively japanese. Ethnic-based national states still remain, as well. In asia and africa, according to Aijaz Ahmad, there is further consolidation of nation-states as mechanisms for regulating markets and revenues. They become sites for the creation of national bourgeoisies and agents in local and regional wars. He also alerts us to the dual processes of the global and the national: an increasing penetration of all available global spaces by capital is accompanied by an intensification of the nation-state form.[30] One need only look at the recent nationalist struggles in eastern europe to see these nation-based manipulations.

Other political analysts argue that the nation-state plays a key role in creating the national policies that attract foreign multinationals.[31] Many east-asian societies are defined by active statist policies. There are multiple varieties: the hyperactivity of the korean state; the mixed laissez-faire stance of Hong Kong.[32] Many third-world states are defined by interventionist, regulatory, juridical, and militarist regimes.[33] Singapore, malaysia, and indonesia, to say nothing of china and vietnam, are strong, centralized, authoritarian states, which also dispense health and welfare provisions, albeit in paternalistic ways. The united states is more privatized than most nations. Meanwhile, the english and french 1997 elections reflect a reclaiming of some of the purpose of the social welfare state. The underwriting of global capital remains a varied subtext of 'the' nation today.

Incredible mobility exists for capital and commodities. Simultaneously, systems of production are fragmented around the globe alongside new transportation technologies.[34] This chaos weakens the nation-state's ability to locate itself economically in a geographical locale. However, the united states and japan have different models for addressing this problem: The u.s. is privatized while japan is state-administered.[35] And, although the united states is pushing to remove restrictions blocking foreign companies from buying and controlling state-run telephone industries, japan and canada reject this move. They remain unwilling to unlock this $602 billion market.[36]

Nevertheless, the imagined globe, free of conflict and power differentials with the nation-state, operates in the cyberimaginings of Nicholas Negroponte, who expects "the nation-state to evaporate." Nations are the wrong size for today. They are not small enough to be local and not large enough to be global. "By the year 2020," he predicts, "the largest employer in the developed world will be the self," displacing both corporation and nation.[37]

This view seems naive at best. The nation-state not only will continue in its twenty-first-century guise enabling transnational corporate growth, it will also deploy itself in new ways to protect "cyberspace's disembodied citizenry." New policies are presently being formulated to regulate "digital identity" for the purpose of surveillance identification.[38] The Clinton administration has also initiated a series of reports on new forms of 'infrastructure terrorism.' It is expected that expenditures in excess of $1 billion by the year 2004 will be necessary for this anti-'terrorist' surveillance of cyberspace.

These expenditures institutionalize the cyber-media complex of transnational capital in its twenty-first-century statist form.[39]

Capitalist Excess and the Globe

Global reorganization of capital means rising prosperity for a few, and rising unemployment and poverty for most of the rest. Some 70 percent of the world's income is produced and consumed by 15 percent of the world's population.[40] This inequity exists within and across nations. More than one-fourth of u.s. workers do not earn wages above the poverty line while CEOs make 149 times as much as an average factory worker. The top 1 percent of u.s. families have more wealth than the entire bottom 90 percent.[41] For workers, economic globalization means deskilling, increased workloads, speed-ups, jobless recoveries, subcontracting, and massive layoffs.[42] It means falling wages for those based in the industrial north.[43] Approximately one-third of the u.s. labor force makes $15,000 or less per year.[44]

According to Jeremy Rifkin, by 2006 only 12 percent of the u.s. workforce will be employed in factories; by 2020, less than 2 percent of the entire global workforce will be.[45] In January 1994, the largest u.s. employers laid off more than 108,000 workers and continue to eliminate more than 2 million jobs each year. From 1985 to 1993, more than three million white collar jobs were scratched. From 1989-93 more than 1.8 million workers lost their jobs in the manufacturing sector. In 1980, u.s.

steel employed 120,000 workers; by 1990, only 20,000 were working. Fifteen percent of people holding jobs for more than one year lost them between 1992 and 1995. Those finding new jobs earned, on average, 14 percent less than previously.[46] Banks have eliminated more than one-third of their workforce by using automatic teller machines.[47] Voice-mail and e-mail have done in thousands more clerical jobs.

This signifies an end to work as it has been known in northern industrial societies. The technological unemployment that began in the 1960s is now devastating the globe. Automation and the global labor pool define the restructuring toward part-time and low-wage service work. Actually, automation is responsible for more layoffs than global relocation, even though the media complex identifies the subhuman foreign worker who survives on substandard wages as the major problem. This harkens back to the displacement of Black cotton laborers: In 1949 only 6 percent of cotton was harvested mechanically, but by 1972 it was completely mechanized. Agricultural and farm robotics define a global agribusiness that holds third-world countries of the south hostage.[48]

This globalized economy has "new geographies of centrality": New York, London, Tokyo, Paris, Hong Kong, Amsterdam, Los Angeles, Buenos Aires, Bangkok, and Mexico City service and finance transnational markets.[49] For Saskia Sassen, the economy is spatially dispersed, but also globally integrated with new forms of centralization. Transterritorial marketplaces are formed.[50] In these relocations, sometimes the center even becomes the periphery.[51] Thus, modern factories are found in vietnam, and sweatshops in Los Angeles.[52] Cities become regional and global nodes in a world economy.[53]

There are an estimated 125,000 garment workers in some 5,000 factories in Los Angeles county. As many as 25 percent are undocumented immigrants. They make up almost 10 percent of u.s. apparel workers and substantiate the "ethnicization of capitalism on a global scale."[54] Even service-sector jobs are being organized sweatshop style. The poor who work these jobs are disproportionately men and women of color. This working class is multiethnic and multiracial, much like the globe itself. They will keep their jobs only as long as they remain competitive with laborers like themselves—but located elsewhere.

An immigrant underclass now defines the meatpacking industry in Nebraska, Iowa, and Kansas. The once lily-white meatpacking communities have become home for impoverished third-world workers. Six hundred mexican and central american workers and 1,500 laotians form the majority of the workforce at the world's second-largest pork factory, operated by Iowa Beef Processors (IBP).[55]

Tens, perhaps hundreds of thousands of immigrants, live in miserable conditions in New York City's Chinatown, Washington Heights, and Queens. On the Lower East Side, chinese immigrants live in tiny bunk rooms akin to animals in a zoo, circa 1950, without hot water or private toilets. Six to ten people often live in a single room. One such immigrant says: "When the mice crawl over us in bed, it feels even more crowded."[56] In Jackson, Mississippi, women still tote water in plastic buckets to bathe their babies.[57]

These realities bespeak the falseness of a clear-cut geographical divide between first and third world. The third world is now at our doorstep, down the block, in the next town over. Yet, new economic extremes also revalue the divide.[58] In response to these boundary changes, a 'fourth-world' even more disadvantaged than the third has emerged in the marginalized economies of third-world rural areas and the shantytowns of african, asian, and latin american cities. Transnational capital views these geographical spaces as throwaway sites, unprofitable for exploitation.[59]

The new extremes of greed affect everyone. Greed cuts through class lines in new ways that affect all first-world workers, working middle class, working poor, and white-collar corporate manager alike. The rich have now become super rich. In 1997 it took a net worth of $475 million, up $60 million from 1996, to get on the Forbes 400 lineup of the ultra-rich.[60] By the early 1990s, 36.9 million were living in poverty in the united states, and 40 percent of the country's poor were children. In 1992, one in ten depended on food stamps and almost half of the poor had jobs with below-poverty wages.[61]

The information economy requires the application of information technology to manufacturing and service industries. We are left with a "lean production" that "maldistributes wealth."[62] More people than ever fear that they will lose their jobs. Others fear that they will never again find another job that can support them and/or their families. Fear and helplessness define people's disposition to the global marketplace. The fear is only heightened by the continued downsizing of social welfare networks for the unemployed and working poor in first-world countries.

Privatized governments leave the poor to fend for themselves while their tax structures assist corporate capital's accumulation. In this antitax era, the very rich get the real tax breaks. In 1945, taxes on the wealthiest americans were as high as 94 percent. During the Reagan years these fell to 50 percent. During the Bush administration, they dropped again to 28 percent.[63] Chart these tax breaks against the enormous profits being earned by those at the top and one sees a clear statement of political advantage for capital accumulation.

In l995, the chief executives at seventy-six of the largest u.s. companies received average salaries of $2 million, up 11 percent since l988.[64] Meanwhile, workers lucky enough to have a job suffered from stagnant incomes. Average weekly earnings for most workers fell by 18 percent between 1973 and 1995, whereas corporate chief executives' pay increased 19 percent—and 66 percent after taxes—from 1979 to 1989.[65] Obviously the global economy works for some, but not most.

Exxon, with profits of $30.9 billion in the past five years, still cut 18,000 jobs in order to stay 'viable'. In this same period, Chevron made $10.2 billion while cutting 9,000 jobs. Mobil made $10.8 billion and cut 8,800 jobs. The North American Free Trade Agreement (NAFTA) lost another 47,000 jobs for the united states, even according to its great defender Robert Reich.[66]

The Gap, a popular middle-class clothes store, uses girls and women in the San Marcos Free Trade Zone in el salvador to produce its clothes. These girls worked compulsory overtime, at 56 cents an hour, for twelve- to fifteen-hour work days while Gap CEO Donald Fisher amassed his personal fortune, to the tune of over $1.5 billion. After a national campaign organized by the National Labor Committee to fight these conditions, the Gap renegotiated its contract with Mandarin International and now pays minimum wage.[67]

Transnational enterprise Nike sells sneakers for up to $140 a pair. Indonesia, where workers earn $2.20 a day, attracted Nike's attention and manufacturing business; so did the wages in vietnam and china, where workers may earn $30 a month. Workers in a factory in Ho Chi Minh City are exposed to carcinogens that exceed local legal standards by 177 times. More than 70 percent of the workers suffer respiratory problems.[68]

Nike's cofounder and current CEO Philip Knight's salary in 1995 was $864,583 plus a $787,500 bonus.[69] His holdings are estimated at over $5 billion. In indonesia, where more than one-third of Nike's products are now made, the minimum wage is $1.25 and many workers live in bamboo or tin dwellings with no running water.[70] Workers, most of whom are women, have few legal rights and often labor under abusive conditions. According to Bob Herbert, of the *New York Times,* Nike will "herald women's rights if it helps sell shoes. And it will stomp on those rights, if it helps to keep the cost down." It obviously "depends on whether the woman is buying their shoes or making them."[71]

May 1993 saw the worst industrial fire in Bangkok's history in a toy factory manufacturing for Toys 'R' Us, Fisher-Price, Hasbro, Tyco, and J. C. Penney. The official toll of the fire was 188 dead and 469 injured. All but fourteen of the dead and injured were young women and girls, most in their early teens.[72] Young girls in the third-world south make toys for children of the first-world north. In this disparate and disturbing sense, the first-world third-world divide still holds. Grave inequity underscores the divide over and over again even as poverty increases on each side.

The toy industry in malaysia, contracted by Mattel toys, makes Statue of Liberty Barbie dolls in factories with little regard for the human rights of their workers.[73] Sewers making Mickey Mouse, Pocahontas, and Lion King toys for Disney in haiti are paid twenty-eight to thirty cents an hour. At the Key-hinge Toy factory in vietnam, Disney characters are made by teenage girls, seven days a week, in wretched conditions. These toys are sold at McDonald's in Happy Meal cartons.[74] Global capitalism has no sense of irony.

Kathie Lee Gifford, the talk-show host with a clothing line for Wal-Mart, was embarrassed by publicity revealing that clothing bearing her name was being produced in sweatshops in haiti and honduras. Meanwhile, much of the children's clothing sold by Disney is produced in burma, despite its military dictatorship. Work weeks are commonly sixty hours, at six cents an hour, which averages out to 48 cents a day, $3.69 a week, and $192 a year.[75]

About half of the clothing sold in the united states is made in asia, central and latin america, and the caribbean. Most of this clothing is made in sweatshops for abysmally low wages. But similar things happen in the united states. In the heart of Los Angeles, seventy thai nationals were discovered sewing clothing for seventeen hours a day at sixty-nine cents an hour.[76]

In response to concerns raised by labor unions and consumers alike, a presidential task force was set up to establish minimum standards for apparel factories in the united states and abroad. A major sticking point was the establishment of minimum wages and maximum hours of work. There was little agreement on what defined a sweatshop as such. Is a sweatshop defined by a sixty-hour week, or the conditions of work, or both? No set minimum wage was agreed on, either. Instead hourly wages vary widely: 26 cents in pakistan; 36 cents in india; 34 cents in indonesia; 62 cents in the philippines; $1.08 in mexico; $5.10 in taiwan; and $5.50 in the united states.[77] No corporation wants to pay more than the going rate, and the u.s. government will not press them.

Capital's Downsizing of Democracy

The culture industries of global capital simultaneously create desire and fear. People crave consumer markets on the one hand, but fear for their jobs on the other. With fewer governmental limits on global capital accumulation, the world gets both meaner and more productive. People gaze at the panoply of consumer choice while their job options seem limited and constraining.

Capitalist markets penetrate and exploit every pocket of available space. The effects are weird yet profitable. The Oklahoma bombing of the federal building created a huge market for anticrime equipment. The O. J. Simpson trial supposedly upped the GNP by $200 million. Prozac, a drug taken to help people cope, adds $1.2 billion to the GDP. Divorce boosts the real estate industry.[78] And while downsizing creates megabucks for a few and unemployment for the rest, it also creates its own consumer markets. Some downsized middle-aged managers are apparently quick to buy a "faux fitness" youth with calf and pectoral implants, lyposuction, face and eye lifts, and hair transplants.[79]

More than 3 million u.s. jobs have been lost to downsizing since 1991.[80] The Fortune 500 firms dropped 4.4 million jobs between 1980 and 1993 even though CEO pay increased more than six-fold. It is very troubling that these developments are part and parcel of the processes that allow a small circle of companies to control more than half of the market in oil, personal computers, and media.[81]

This particular concentration of power distorts the power realities of displaced labor. Global capital's excesses are routed in and through the telecommunications complex, which controls what is shown to the public. Media-ted and real lose their borders; hyppereal occludes the exploitation, much like the economic nation is vaporized.

'Downsizing,' the twenty-first century's version of firing, recodes the struggle between labor and capital as one between global competitiveness and nation-state sluggishness.[82] Language matters here. Downsizing, as a term, has been neutralized; when one downsizes one is simply streamlining and reconstituting, not unfairly increasing profits at the expense of working people. Actually, the downsized worker is fired to further enhance corporate excess. However, "fired" sounds too harsh. When you are fired, you are allowed to be angry. When you are downsized, you are expected to be understanding. It is no one's fault. It is a global necessity, and the globe is just too big and unreal to blame.

Downsizing has become the mantra of neoliberal economic theory. It is seen as a necessity, rather than as an unfair restructuring of capital accumulation free of governmental controls or public debate. It operates in the market to streamline and eliminate labor while it covers over its deliberate effect of inequity and excess.[83]

Downsizing operates politically as an antigovernment discourse that justifies privatizing once-public spheres and activities. Global capital wants it all: to extend its markets into public parks, public schools, garbage collection. It is a pay-as-you-go plan. Big business makes money all around, and the CEOs get to take their money and run.

Downsized governments tax the rich less while the middle classes absorb the tax burden. Given the smaller tax base, the poor are forced to absorb the loss of governmental subsidies, and they must adjust to the dismantling of the public services on which they depended. Many u.s. cities have cut back bus service for lack of funds. Some public transportation systems, as in Greenville, South Carolina, have been completely shut down and the poor, the elderly, and the handicapped have been left stranded.[84] In Montgomery, Alabama, site of the historic civil rights boycott, bus service was cut in half and people without cars have a hard time getting to work. Racialized class inequalities are reinscribed as governmental responsibility is whittled away.

Media depiction of downsizing most often does not uncover the underlying power struggle. The *New York Times* ran a week-long series on downsizing and tracked its effect on white, high-paid managerial men.[85] The series ignored the middle working classes, the working poor, women, and people of color. Some white-collar managers are clearly in jeopardy today, but they comprise a small part of the problem. If the real effects of downsizing—the eventual displacement of labor for a majority of workers across the globe—are shown then the so-called necessities of transnational capital look different. If downsizing is shown to be in the interest of a very few and the disinterest of 'the rest of us' its defense is undermined. The excess is uncovered as indecent.

The stunning effect of these transforming times hits every kind of worker: white collar, blue collar, pink collar, no collar, professional/nonprofessional. They all make up what has come to be loosely thought of as the middle class. In europe, where 11 percent of available workers are already unemployed, the swiftness and size of the job cuts are straining families and communities.[86] As the structure of work in the information age changes, expressions of class anger emerge in disparate forms.

Pat Buchanan tapped into this anger in his 1996 presidential bid when he railed against both big government and big business.[87] Although some people are beginning to think that big business takes too much for itself, this does not come full circle to a critique of global capital. Rather, enemies are constructed through old regimes of fear and hate. In the united states, immigrants are blamed. Or the workers in the philippines who work for too little. Or welfare recipients who supposedly ballooned the deficit.

This kind of blaming is not, however, the whole story. Workers in the Hoover Company plant in North Canton, Ohio, rejected a proposal to create a lower tier of wages for new hires ($7.50 an hour versus $14.50) even though Hoover threatened to go to a nonunion plant in El Paso, Texas. Bob Black, a twenty-five-year veteran at Hoover responded: "It's like they want to eliminate the middle class."[88] Black knew he had to protect these new hires or there would be little left for any of them.

The more people lose their jobs, or work several in order to come up with their former wages, one would hope that excessive corporate profits would seem less acceptable. Nearly three-fourths of all u.s. households have had some experience with layoffs since 1980. About one-third have had at least one member of their family lose a job.[89] Yet, even though people express individual upset at their own plight, there is little sense of collective anger. More often than not, people feel isolated and alone when they lose their job, which is a long way from feeling a sense of class solidarity.

Instead of jobs, consumer culture provides people with escape. Disneyland, shopping malls, t.v. soaps, and tabloids assist us in losing our memory and our thoughts. Stores are stocked to the ceilings leaving one to wonder who has the money to buy the stuff.

Privatization and commercialization of public life affect all facets of everyday life in unexpected ways. State parks have little or no budget for repairs, life-guards, or garbage collection. Heavy snows and federal cutbacks created a two-week delay in opening the Bear Tooth scenic highway in Montana in 1996, and the tourist town of Red Lodge unexpectedly lost millions in revenue.[90] These unintended consequences have their own ripple effect.

The downsizing of government, along with labor, delivers a double-whammy to the poor *and* middle classes that have become dependent on the public sector. These stresses cut across and through racialized class lines. On the other side are private, suburban, gated communities that cater to white upper-middle-class separatism.

People commute longer distances to work and have less time for familial responsibilities. Families often live apart due to job location. Other families split apart over the stresses of money and unemployment.[91] People feel more alone and in competition with each other because they are. A widower with two children says "Not only will you have to look for jobs anywhere in the U.S., but in Singapore and Hong Kong. . . . And you're also competing against kids from other countries."[92] Competitors exist everywhere.

The loss of a job often also means the loss of health-care benefits, so that one lives in fear of an accident requiring medical treatment. Some parents will not let children play school sports because they could break a leg and the parents could not afford to pay the bill.

This framing of excessive individualism—that those who have more get it because they deserve it, and the rest must work harder—demands a new covenant not only between global capital, first-world national governments, and families, but also between individuals and the companies they work for. The company no longer conceives of itself as the paternalist father who takes care of his own. In the past, this paternalism was more often the ideal than the reality, but today it is no longer even an ideal.

Since the early 1970s, the company has shed its paternal pretense and has become a child in the global market, heeding the all-powerful transnational father. Companies are helpless and no longer helpful. Corporatist familialism has been downsized by the global necessities.[93] Global capital, no matter its heterogeneity, now shifts its discourse of responsibility from the company *and* the nation to a form of fantasized self-help familialism.

In reality, families, although sometimes havens, more often reflect the world around them. They are in disarray, much like governments themselves, in part because of external pressures, and in part because of the internal contradictions of patriarchal family life. Women, who are held responsible for family life, face the demands of everyday life with less help. There is less time, less money, and less community.

Yet, food still gets prepared, and water hauled, and laundry washed and dried. Women continue to do an enormous amount of child care. They are the ones who usually provide for elderly parents. This happens alongside unforgiving poverty, lost jobs, dismantled governments, and structural adjustment programs enforced by the International Monetary Fund (IMF) and World Bank. Global capital operates as freely as it does today because of the collaborative impotence of first-world nation-states and the continued potency of women's familial labor.

Postnations and Virtual Globes

Electronic mediation combined with mass migration creates what Appadurai terms "new diasporic public spheres," which transcend individual nations and become the "crucibles of a postnational political order."[94] These postnational publics sometimes allow for identities that are not simply territorial or nation-based.[95] Women's feminist dialogues constitute the most promising postnational public that I can see. From our unique positioning as familial and wage laborers, we might be able to see through and past the racialized class divisions of the globe.

The mobility of modern life can require living in one country while one's heart is tied to another. E-mail allows one alternative homes—or multiple ones, for that matter. The process of moving is central to our world; it promises both opportunity and suffering. As identity becomes more portable and fluid, different notions of the 'nation' become possible. The speed at which information travels allows for both the disruption of former identities, nations, and families AND their reconstitution.[96]

To move beyond the nation to a dialogue that does not enhance the rights of global capital, we must embrace a commitment to public life and democratic community. Moving beyond the nation, but with a sense of public responsibility for one another, demands limits to the power of transnational capital AND bureaucratic statism, while retaining a notion of democracy that moves beyond the consumer-self to a deliberative notion of individual collectivity—where both the individual *and* the collective are recognized with distinct needs.

Disparate and sporadic stirrings have already begun that may mobilize activities in this direction. In the wake of the successful UPS strike, the union movement is hopefully beginning to revive. The people of iran, especially young people and women of all ages, voted in large numbers for Mohammed Khatami, choosing to relax a restrictive Islamic fundamentalism in favor of "increased freedom" and participation.[97] Carolyn Browner, head of the Environmental Protection Agency stands firmly for the Clean Air Act and remains determined to toughen air-quality standards. The outcry in argentina against rising unemployment and free-market policy increases. Argentinian college students are demanding renewed social spending for national education. A european postponement of the offensive against the social welfare state may have begun with the election of Tony Blair in england and with strikers and demonstrators in france continuing to demand better jobs.[98] The south korean labor movement is growing and in 1995 established the Korean Confederation of Trade Unions (KCTU).[99]

Governing, in the information age of transnational capital, assists privatized individualism. It remains to be seen what a newly invented notion of government—one that effectively governs capital and its racialized patriarchal priorities—might look like. This revisioned notion of government must clearly recognize and blend individuality and publicness, protect the rights of workers, provide access to information, build a democracy that includes people of color and women of all colors, and nurture the richness of differences that constitute any community.

A Twenty-First-Century Political Contract

Former labor secretary Robert Reich challenged u.s. workers to take a stand. First he said: "Do not blame corporations and their top executives. . . . If we want them to put greater emphasis on the interests of their workers and communities, society must reorganize them to do so."[100] But he sounds less sanguine after his tenure in the Clinton administration. In his memoir, *Locked in the Cabinet,* Reich laments the powerlessness of workers and the rule of Wall Street and the pentagon.[101]

Workers' needs are silenced while corporate capital expects the state to nurture its needs. NAFTA and GATT enabled global corporations to establish the regional—as opposed to national—agreements necessary for their success. Changes in tariff and tax law further increased profits. Transnational corporations, with help from their nation-states, have become more powerful than many governments.[102]

The telecommunications media heralded the post-1989 triumph of capital from the start. Transnational media reinforce the sense that this global process is universal and inevitabile. Yet, through some of these same media sources, we receive a glimmer of dissent: the Zapatistas in Chiapas denouncing NAFTA as a swindle for mexican workers; Bob Herbert's *New York Times* editorial decrying the outrageous profits of Nike; news reports about women gathering in Beijing, china, to demand that governments end sex discrimination. John Sweeney, former president of the AFL-CIO tells the Los Angeles Board of Supervisors that if it pushes through a plan to cut 18,000 workers from its payroll, his union will conduct a "massive campaign of resistance and retribution."[103] These voices are disparate, and few and far between, but they are also beginning to mobilize new support.

Health care workers, hospital executives, and union officials finally came together to protest the proposed Republican cutbacks in current spending on Medicare and Medicaid.[104] A new group called Working Today is attempting to create an employee lobby of all types of workers: "all those who work or want to work—professionals, service workers, managers and time-clock punchers, consultants, part-time and seasonal workers, and the unemployed." They intend to design an internet strategy to connect "downsized managers with part-time hamburger flippers."[105]

The National Labor Committee continues to monitor and criticize sweatshop labor wherever it exists. After a six-month campaign against the Gap and Mandarin International, the Committee was able to get the Gap to agree to independent third-party monitoring of its overseas contract operations.

If the twenty-first century is to be defined by progressive democracies, transnational capital will have to be downsized and held accountable by the different publics it affects. New notions of enabling governments will have to be constructed alongside new conceptions of deliberative public life. The u.s. government—as it presently exists—can no longer simply be activated. The past quarter-century of privatization has corrupted it too deeply.

If the nation is to stake out a claim for publicness new publics must speak out and press for their voices to be heard. These voices cannot pander to consumerism or the culture industries that sustain it. These publics must formulate and name the diverse desires and needs of the communities that inhabit the globe. Both shared collectivity and unique individuality must be nurtured and respected. The connections across the globe must be understood and recognized along with their indigenous and authentic cultural origins. These communities must be renegotiated in nonracist and nonsexist form.

Curbs and limits must be set on global capital. At present, there are only small and disconnected attempts to initiate this process.

Scrap the lack of individual/sexual freedom in cuba, but let's embrace its free medical care. Let's carefully think through cuba's policy on foreign investment, which allows investment in all sectors of the economy except health, education, and the armed forces.[106] Let's follow cuba's guarantee of a liter of milk a day for twenty-five cents for all children up to the age of fourteen, the sick, and the elderly.

We can also learn from denmark's free public health care system, which is paid through taxes. The cost of its system is 6.5 percent of GNP, less than half the relative cost in the united states. Danes think the u.s. system creates too much waste through inefficient private bureaucracy and the surplus earnings of doctors, insurance companies, and hospital corporations.[107]

The economic poverty of africa and racist media distortions of its rich cultural traditions blind much of the rest of the globe to africa's alternative visions. Africa is another starting place for rethinking democracy and markets for the twenty-first century. Grace Lee Boggs notes the "revolution of Self-Reliance" that defines much of africa today. This is an incredible struggle "to end hunger, protect the environment and achieve self-reliance by planting trees, diversifying cereal, fruit and vegetable crops, and building village granaries."[108] This notion of self-reliance is not built on bourgeois individualism but rather as part of an invigorating communal and social life. Self-reliance is a defiant stance against global capital's intervention AND a progressive embrace of environmental preservation.

Subsaharan africa boasts tens of thousands of these self-reliance grassroot groups. Women are in the majority and provide leadership in these grassroots actions. The large number of africans involved in the struggle for self-reliance reject 'victim status' and instead say they must try to make a difference.

They see themselves building a movement, individual by individual, through small groups networking with each other.

These peasant movements embrace hope. They are committed to freeing the world from hunger. To do this, they employ an hybrid strategy which celebrates african identity but in twenty-first-century ways. They struggle for a "cultural rootedness" but with a global perspective that includes "the wonderful diversity of our oneness."[109]

Women in vietnam, india and bangladesh now own and run small enterprises related to the needs of everyday life that can teach collectivity alongside individual initiative. Privatization in limited sectors need not mean a wholesale endorsement of consumer culture. As women take hold of new opportunities, but maintain their local communal roots, new imaginings across place are possible and desirable.

Too few north americans have heard of the "Seventeen Principles of Environmental Justice" adopted by three-hundred African-American, Native American, Latino, and Asian-American delegates at the First National People of Color Environmental Leadership Summit, held in October 1991.[110] Participants examined the environmental racism of toxins and pollutants, which disproportionately affect their communities. Individual health is a central concern of this public agenda.

A revolutionary twenty-first-century political contract is needed to protect the environment and water and wood supplies, guarantee a livable wage for each individual, provide free and available health care including reproductive freedom, recognize individuality and freedom of speech, and guarantee access to education and the modes of communication. Such a contract would begin the process of articulating the indecency

of transnational capital and its racialized/sexualized consumerist culture.

This might sound like a dream-world. But in this highly
media-ted information world, it is more politically important
than ever to dream.

5
wishing/hoping

Transnational Capitalist Patriarchy, Beijing,
and Virtual Sisterhoods

wishing/hoping

Global capital thrives because of a racial-patriarchal transnational sexual division of labor. In other words, capitalist
transnational corporations orchestrate a division of labor that
disproportionately locates women and girls, especially those of
color, in low-wage assembly and information jobs and in sexual
ghettoes elsewhere in the market. Meanwhile, women are still
expected to continue rearing children and performing familial
labor.

Women constitute half of humanity, but they remain the
poorest of the poor. They do approximately two-thirds of the
world's work and earn about one-tenth of its income. They own
less than s hundredth of its property.[1] Women make up a majority of the world's refugees. They search for firewood and
water in degraded environments. They are pushed into prostitution.[2] Across enormous differences in culture, geography,

134

and wealth, they suffer from domestic violence, and sexual slavery. A universal patriarchal domination prevails. Of course, male privilege does not exist in the same way everywhere, but rather mimics as well as reforms local prejudice to its own needs.

Transnational capitalist patriarchy, as a series of powerful economic, sexual, and racial relationships, attempts to rationalize and modernize traditional masculinist hierarchy. In this process, the consumer culture of the cyber-media complex sells images and fantasies that have little to do with the real world of women or men. The market forces of capital often conflict with the familial role of women: porn and prostitution exist alongside traditional families in thailand, russia, the united states, and elsewhere; women's wage labor exists alongside the sexual division of labor both inside and outside the market.

Transnational capital has no one agenda for patriarchy. Rather, it deploys different strategies in different cultural settings. As a result, in the twenty-first century, new extremes of rich and poor will create more economic inequality among women as a whole. Yet, the sexual division of labor that assigns childbearing/rearing and domestic labor to women applies cross-culturally and produces significant similarities in women's lives. Motherhood remains the domain of women. This likeness is then economically differentiated by the increasing amounts of wage labor done by women in factories, in information centers, and as sex workers. The poverty of women in the third-world south, and of women of the south living in the north, creates a new geography of capitalist patriarchal power. The sexual division of labor is rewritten with the extremes of global capital.

Family and transnational capital compete for women's labor. Just as the nuclear family has replaced the extended family in most first-world countries, today the nuclear family of husband and wife is displaced by single-parent families. As first-world nations privatize, they call upon the fantasized family of yesteryear; as third-world countries supply export industry, they unsettle traditional patriarchal familial parameters.

The needs of transnational capital thus often undermine aspects of patriarchy, much like capitalist markets have always done. But now, first-world nation-states exacerbate these tensions, whereas vietnam and china continue paternalist policies as their countries industrialize. The patriarchal relations of the cyber/media complex both enable AND disable the semi-autonomous relations of global capitalism and its racialized patriarchal commitments.

Just as transnational capital appeared triumphant across the globe, women gathered in Beijing in 1995 to say their needs were not being met.[3] Speakers at the conference appeared on CNN, calling for a democracy that envisioned the protection of the environment, an end to sexual violence and sexual trafficking of girls and women, the right to reproductive control, and world peace.

This moment in Beijing starkly contrasts with the privatized and individualist global discourses of the day. Women gathered and said, for all the world to hear, that governments throughout the five continents must commit to ending sex discrimination and act affirmatively on behalf of women's rights. Women reminded the world of the need for a publicness that envisions the earth as a home, and the home, not as women's sphere, but as a human habitat.[4]

It makes perfect sense that women would want to speak across their differences and as one voice at this particular time. The global economy, with its racialized and sexualized contours, redeploys patriarchy in 'new-old' ways. The *re*privatization of patriarchy in first-world-north countries relocates women's burden to their single-parent status and/or their double day of labor. The consolidation of global capital's power leaves women doing more, as third-world governments defer to the World Bank and the IMF.[5] These renegotiations rearrange public and private domains.

It is less clear why the Beijing meeting was publicized for all the world to see. Why did CNN choose to cover the conference in the first place? CNN brought this news story to people around the world, exposing women's exploited living conditions and their outrage about them at the same time. Is this just the cyber/media complex at its best—allowing talk to seem like REAL action while governments are free to do nothing?

Although CNN coverage of the Beijing conference was what one might expect—with the 'official' story told by U.N. representatives, lots of time for Hillary Clinton's speech, and very little focus on the Non-Governmental Organizations (NGOs) meeting at Huairou—it was not news as usual. So which parts of this story are subversive of the media/consumer culture complex and which are not?

Obviously, I am wondering about the absorption of women's feminist agendas by the consumer industries. Were women being taken seriously in the news reporting of Beijing, or were women's interests just being marketed? I am also wondering which aspects of Beijing's agenda cannot be absorbed and vaporized by the very cyber/media U.N. complex that hosted the conference. The e-mail networking during and after the conference allowed for complex and multiple dialogues beyond the confines of the original meetings. Importantly, though, the majority of the world's women are not online.

Listserves for women establish e-mail networks among angola, south africa, ecuador, chile, bangladesh, china, australia, and so on. Dialogue and information travel between and through enormous geographical and cultural divides, though the divides also remain. The telecom-cyber complex provides potential sources of liberatory democracy alongside the super-exploitation of women. While some women draw water and scratch out subsistence lives, others develop e-mail networks with women around the world. Nothing remains as separate or contained as it once was.

Given that telecommunications technologies mean different things for different women, I need to trace their different paths: from computer terminals that surveil them at work, to prodemocracy internet sites, to e-mail correspondence between israeli and palestinian women, to expressions of net feminisms. This is actually part of a much larger story with an even longer history: the process by which capitalist technologies unsettle established forms of patriarchy in favor of more modern ones. Global capital and its technologies begin to undo some of the very power relations it depends on even as it repositions these racialized patriarchal relations in post-modern form.

Seeing and Not-Seeing 'Real' Women and Girls

Women of the first-world north and west are used to symbolize and transmit consumerist freedom and cultural allure on the global screen.[6] Media sexually objectify women and use violent gender imagery to subdue messages of freedom. The 'urban-centric' focus of news misrepresents women elsewhere. Because media imagery is such an influential site of representation, it remains a site of contestation and debate between nations and across the globe.[7]

The very technologies that constitute these telecommunications networks—such as the net and e-mail—can allow women to build "a new kind of global alternative public sphere." Unlikely possibilities do exist, like the playful use of western videos by women in "some traditional societies to open up their private spheres to new images which patriarchal cultures still seek to control."[8] So sexually explicit materials can be used in private by women for their own purposes while constraining traditional modes still define public domains.

Yet, new computer technology displaces female labor, reorganizes it to new sites, and/or increases the poverty of women and girls. For women, transnational capital, with its high-tech global telecommunications systems, is contradictory—alienating *and* potentially liberatory. Capable of enormous levels of exploitation for the majority of women and girls, it also promises a new transnational but postpatriarchal deliberative democracy built by women across the globe.

In pakistan 15 percent of women are in the labor force and some 24 percent are illiterate. In nicaragua 32 percent of women are in the labor force and abortion is illegal. In sri lanka 31 percent of women are in the labor force and 87 percent are illiterate, and abortion is illegal.[9]

About 585,000 women die every year from pregnancy-related causes—one every minute. Eighteen million women suffer debilitating diseases and injuries related to childbirth. Maternal mortality and morbidity continue to be a key problem around the globe.

More than half a billion women live in complete poverty outside the formal global economy. Hundreds of millions cannot read or write.[10] Tens of thousands of asian children are exploited in brothels in cambodia, india, china, thailand, the philippines, and taiwan.[11] An estimated 1 million child prostitutes, mostly girls, work in asia.[12] Half of the world's malnourished children live in bangladesh, india, and pakistan.[13] In Bombay one-third of the city's 20 million are homeless. Given the city's sex industry, it is expected that AIDS will kill at least ten thousand people a month in the near future, many of these young girls and boys.[14]

Huge numbers of women and girls are forced migrants and refugees—in bosnia, angola, rwanda, haiti, and other countries. They comprise almost 80 percent of displaced persons in africa, asia, and latin america. Two-thirds of the total refugee population in somalia were women.[15] In bosnia, 80 percent of the 23 million refugees uprooted by the violence were women.[16]

The numbers of poor are increasing, and women make up 70 percent of those living in poverty worldwide. In 1993, 34,000 children were dying each day in need of food and/or medical supplies.[17] Poverty, illiteracy, and sexual violence top the list of major problems facing women.

Subsaharan africa has some of the lowest literacy levels with about 43 percent of women literate. In latin america and the caribbean, literacy rates are much higher, often climbing to 85 percent.[18]

Despite the poverty, most women, according to Gertrude Mongella, assistant secretary-general of the Fourth World Conference on Women in Beijing, are "efficient managers of scarce resources and capable entrepreneurs."[19] They hold the key to economic development in their own countries. They spend their days growing food, gathering firewood, carrying water, and cooking, even as they work to build their own futures.[20] Their daily domestic duties discipline them in unique ways.

Global capital, now homeless, has new fluidity for exploitation. The locations of women's exploitation multiply as women and girls come to make up more than half the labor force in most countries and continue to labor as housewives, mothers, and domestics. Or, as Claudia von Werlhof says, "the proletarian is dead; long live the housewife" who must claim not only her labor, but her body, her land, her children, and her house.[21] The global capitalist-patriarchal model of accumulation *re*discovers and intensifies women's domesticity alongside wage labor.[22]

The flexibility of women's labor—in its domestic, informal, and unregulated invisible dimension—remains a continual resource for transnational capital. The arena of invisible/unrecognized domestic labor is repositioned against paid work. While women continue to grow food and secure water and fuel supplies, they also make up some 80 percent of the workforce of export-oriented manufacture.[23]

Paid work spans a wide spectrum for women: home-based workers, migrants, factory workers, rural farmers, service workers, and professionals.[24] In the united states, the AFL-CIO has begun to recognize the importance of women's labor for the union movement. By 1996, women accounted for 39 percent of all union members. They constitute the poorest of workers, with two-thirds in part-time work and half in temporary jobs.[25]

In asia, some 375 million landless female laborers perform the menial chores such as weeding, hoeing, and milking. In africa, women produce 78 percent of the continent's food. In the united states, 75 percent of poverty is concentrated among women, a majority of whom have jobs and are also mothers. Across these vast geographical distances, the informalization of labor continues. Unregulated sweatshops, in the form of textiles and electronics work farmed out to women in the home as a new form of industrial homeworking, flourish alongside unpaid domestic labor.[26]

Privatization of government services disproportionately affects women because of their poverty and status as mothers. The context for much of women's labor—underpaid and unpaid—is perpetuated and condoned by international financial institutions such as the World Bank and the International Monetary Fund (IMF). Privatization policy, especially in debt-ridden third-world countries, articulates national agendas set by global capital.[27] Privatization policy places disproportionate burdens on women by reducing the very services they need: education, health care, and child care, each of which allows them to stay on the job. Without welfare payments, 70 percent of all single mothers with young children in the netherlands would fall into poverty.[28]

The unrecognized and invisible domestic labor of women sustains the grid on which much governmental privatization relies.[29] These invisibilities further reproduce the inequities of first-world service-sector work and third-world factory labor among women and girls. These women become the consumers for that which they produce, but as "subsistence reproducers."[30]

Home-based work further confounds the intricacies of the public/private divide for women. Women, as home-based workers, are self-employed in the informal sectors of the economy. These workers are pulled into industrial production, which is subcontracted to the home.[31] The mexican and argentinian garment industries subcontract to home-based workers in the countryside. These arrangements are spreading to india and taiwan.[32] This new 'flexible' production redefines the place of work and, with it, the relations defining family and labor. As family/labor and private/public collapse in on each other, traditional forms of patriarchal hierarchy are undermined. For some women, this work allows a new access to resources and respectability, which confronts more traditional patriarchal relations.

Home-based work is not regulated by the government in india. Ninety-four percent of women workers in india work in the informal sector, where capital can operate free of labor laws and state agencies.[33] Home-based *bidi* workers in india have been forced to become self-employed so their former bosses no longer have to abide by labor regulations. This apparent 'flexibility' is exploitative.

Home-based industrial work is not limited to the philippines, malaysia, or india. It is establishing itself in first-world northern countries as well. In Prairie Hills, Iowa, and Riverton, Wisconsin, home-based assembly work is seen as a viable development strategy for General Motors. The company exploits the secondary and supplemental status of women's labor by restructuring portions of the automotive assembly process to female home-based workers, who are already tied to the home and have few options to leave.[34] Women's outsider status, as tied to home, makes them a flexible alternative to capital investment.

Privatization of governments redirects labor to the home. In part, this relocation displaces and rewires engendered labor within transnational economies from public to familial spaces. Women, as home-based workers, become doubly invisible: as unpaid domestic laborers and as exploited industrial workers. Home-based work deepens patriarchal hierarchies while sidestepping the nation-state and also undermining the traditional, male-dominated family hierarchy. But this sexual division of labor is also a part of the same masculinist privilege that relegates women to the low-paid rungs of the service and factory sectors of the global economy.[35]

This is a pretty good deal for transnational corporations and the men who run them. Women's "low paid and unpaid labour is the foundation of the modern economy and society."[36] Transnational capitalist patriarchy wants it all: it wants women's labor as wives, housewives (which is not meant as a western construct but rather bespeaks women's domesticity, whether on the land or in the house), and child rearers—*and* as low paid workers.[37] As a result, women around the globe work 13 percent more hours than men.[38]

Electronic and garment factories head to export-oriented zones for cheap(er) labor. Seventy-five percent of the workers used in these zones are girls and women aged sixteen to twenty-four. Supposedly these jobs represent a way out of subsistence farming and traditional family relations. But this is another instance of the shifting location of patriarchal relations: the export factory of the global market is a new patriarchal site for third-world-south countries.[39] Many of the girls and women working in the maquiladora factories do so because it is their only option as the global market pushes them off the land.[40]

Nike, Adidas, and L.A. Gear are notorious for their use of women workers in free-trade zones. Korean women, who organized for better wages, were quickly replaced by women in central america and indonesia.[41] The Mandarin international sweatshop in the San Marcos free-trade zone paid fifty-six cents an hour with work days extending to eighteen hours.[42] Wanija Timornrum works in the Dynamic Toy Factory in Bangkok, making Lion King and Mickey Mouse dolls. Her wage is roughly five dollars a day. She took the job about twenty years ago, at age seventeen.[43]

The maquiladora workers work from midnight to 7 P.M., with twenty minutes for lunch. During rush orders, they work twenty-three-hour shifts. The young girls who wish to finish school cannot do so. These girls say that their bosses scream at them all the time; demand they finish their quotas before they are allowed to leave; will only give two toilet breaks; and require that they take birth control pills, telling them that they are for malaria.[44]

Women also make up a majority of the workers in clothing factories around the world, many of which are sweatshops. Average hourly wages range from 7 cents in bangladesh to 20 cents in china, 22 cents in nicaragua, 29 cents in indonesia, and 1 dollar in the united states.[45] Women today predominate in garment, textile, toy, and electronics assembly lines throughout the third world.

More and more women are now working at computer terminals filing insurance claims and airline tickets. In barbados, women enter three hundred thousand ticket reservations flowing from two thousand daily flights for one u.s. airline. Other women enter data for american medical insurance claims. Information-processing computer terminals in jamaica, st. kitts, haiti, china, and singapore connect other sites across the globe.[46]

The GNP in thailand and the philippines is significantly bolstered by prostitution, the main growth industry fueling tourism. Thai, filipino, and sri lankan domestic workers are sent to east asia, the middle east, and first-world-north countries, where they are severely exploited and sexually abused. The philippines exports sixty thousand female domestic workers to Hong Kong; the singapore government reaps $234 million annually from the maid levy.[47] The sexual exploitation of girls and women continues to be a significant resource for patriarchal social relations.

Women's labor is subjected to new forms of technology that increase the pauperization of women. Their jobs are either low-wage or no-wage.[48] When women do get jobs that give them access to income that is not tied to the sex trade, these jobs begin to undermine the traditional patriarchal familial relations that maintain transnational capital. This unsettling of traditional patriarchal forms applies to industrial and agricultural countries alike.

Add together—in geometric form—the modernizing challenges of capital, the media-cyber complex of consumerism (which both establishes and undermines sexism), and the telecommunications technologies that let us see and talk across the globe, and we can begin to imagine the possibility, however small, of challenging the masculinist privilege of global capital.

Family Politics and Nation-States

Government provisions for public welfare, public education, public health; for legal protections against sexual and racial discrimination; for safeguarding the environment and enforcing clean air standards, are in demise in most first-world countries. Women and girls, given their unique status in the divisions of labor are hardest hit.

Before the privatization of the social welfare state, women in countries like the united states and sweden had their needs partially met through state programs: food stamps, day-care provisions, educational opportunity programs, infant health care, and so on. The dismantling of these programs—paternalist as they were—through the 1980s has had particularly devastating consequences on the health and welfare of family life.

Most women have few alternatives to the service-oriented, high-tech, minimum-wage jobs available today. These low-wage jobs cannot sustain a family's needs, especially if there are young children in need of day-care. The problem of divorce—and single-parent families—further complicates the underclass status of women across the globe. Thirty-five percent of households in the caribbean are headed by women as are 21 percent in latin america, 20 percent in subsaharan africa, 13 percent in north african and west asia.[49] The low wages paid to women in free-trade zones and service economies cannot support single-parent households.

Several third-world industrializing countries such as vietnam appear to be concerned with a notion of public health and family planning. It remains to be seen whether these commitments will continue against the constant pressure of transnational capital. One group, Alternative Women in Development (AWID), writes in defense of this notion of publicness: "There is an important role for government to play in bringing about a society which meets people's basic needs and is just, peaceful, and environmentally sound." Governments have a responsibility to achieve the "common good" and this requires regulating corporate power and eliminating gross income inequality.[50] In this view, jobs and health are rights that must be protected and nurtured, not simply exploited.

Given the pressures placed upon women's lives, it should be no surprise that women are more supportive than men of the social welfare state.[51] U.S. delegates to the Beijing conference returned home to set up a "Contract With American Women" to implement the *Platform for Action* adopted at the conference. The contract calls for ending the burden of poverty, affordable and good quality health care, sexual and reproductive rights, the sharing of family responsibilities, educational equity, protecting the environment, and ending violence against women.[52] A renewed contract between the nation-state and its women attempts to retrieve the social welfare component of publicness on behalf of women and their families.

Not surprisingly, little if anything is heard—in the news, on CNN, from President Clinton—about this contract. Instead, the social welfare state is demonized time and time again. In this scenario welfare women play a mythic role that has little to do with the 'facts.' Women on welfare are used to epitomize everything wrong with first-world nation-state governments: they are bloated, incompetent, and a drain on everyone else. The media depict Black women as having too much sex and too many babies, living high off the rest of 'us.' The programs that supposedly support this deviant behavior are then easily scrapped.[53]

The 'facts' no longer count for much. Image is everything. Few people seem to think it matters that Aid to Families with Dependent Children (AFDC) benefits are less than 1 percent of the federal budget; that the typical welfare family is a white mother with two children; that more than 50 percent of those on welfare only remain on it for two years; that full-time, year-round work at minimum wage puts a woman and her two children three thousand dollars below the poverty line, with no health-care provisions. In June 1996, the House of Representatives adopted the welfare reform plan pioneered in Wisconsin, which eliminated welfare and Medicaid entitlements. A year later, welfare as it had been known in the united states also ended. Meanwhile, the post-Beijing contract languishes.

Republican women senators, on the whole, supported the welfare-slashing reform packages. They see government as failed and reject its role as a provider of services and protector of equal rights.[54] They wish to redress the welfare state's undermining of traditional patriarchal relations to the extent that it enables nontraditional family forms. The *re*privatized state smashes the progressive effects of social welfare and renews the discourse of individual achievement and responsibility. 'The' family becomes a cover, once again, for establishing new forms of patriarchal privilege.

Women's secondary status is cohesively articulated through their placement in the global market alongside their identification with family. Women's status is simultaneously mirrored in and through media-ted viewings of the racialized consumerist culture. There is little linear or coherent about these processes. This is especially true once we recognize the prevalence of female-headed households made up of mothers and their children. In addition, out-of-wedlock births are becoming more common around the globe. They first doubled and then tripled in the last twenty years in europe.[55]

Transnational capital exacerbates and rearticulates sexual hierarchy in the market alongside female-headed households. It is not yet clear what the outcome of these revisioned masculinist relations among family, nation-state, global economy, and consumer culture will be. Female-headed families begin to undermine the sites of male privilege, while consumer culture continually recaptures them. The geographical boundaries of the economic nation have shifted to create a crisis of political authority. Privatized nation-states demand more labor and sustenance of family life. Yet, families are on their own with old rules for new circumstances.

Politicians, at least since Ronald Reagan, seem more comfortable talking about family and family values than about the economy. Even Bill Clinton, who in 1992 was famous for saying "it's the economy, stupid," adopted "family issues" as his 1996 campaign strategy. "Neofeminist" Naomi Wolf assisted with this strategy, convincing Clinton that he needed to be a comforting authority figure, "who builds and then defends the family home."[56] At one point in the 1996 campaign, Hillary even told the nation that she was thinking of another child, that maybe she would adopt one. Bill Clinton focused on issues like teen curfews, the need for uniforms in schools, and the V-chip to protect children from violence on t.v.

Governing becomes more implicated with the culture industries as the cyber-media complex becomes more dominant. Patriarchal consumer culture capitalizes on Clinton as 'the' good father (he clearly is *not* the good husband) while he tries to smooth over shifting locations of patriarchal/racialized privilege. He calls for an open dialogue on race and tells the nation we must learn to live together across racial difference, but he does nothing to put new antiracist policy in place.

The hyperreal works in loose fashion here. The arenas of economy, racialized nation, and family disarrange and recombine. The 'good white father' reasserts racialized male privilege just by being the president. First-world transnation-states reposition the symbolic of patriarchy: masculinist privilege becomes further disconnected from its traditionalist moorings while utilizing the hyperreal.

The mythic economic nation-state is displaced by the imaginary family and by self-help rhetoric. Twenty-first-century privatization of first-world nation-states depends on these fantasies, no matter how un-real they are. The 'idea' of family has always had enormous psychic resonance because, in part, it means that we are not alone. Global capital just may undermine the salience of the mythic family to the point that people look for connection elsewhere. The grisly nationalist wars of the late twentieth century might be a part of this complicated narrative.

The attempt to humanize and 'feminize' the state constitutes another, more peaceful scenario of this familial narrative. This may be why the swedes in 1994 elected the most female government in the world: women will make politics more like a family, more caring. Sadly, women are being elected just as the kindness of government is shrinking.[57]

Women are also making inroads into state legislatures in the united states. Four out of every ten seats in the Washington state legislature are filled by women. In Arizona and Colorado, women legislators are forcing debate on maternity leave, domestic violence, and divorce law. These legislators speak out against cuts in social services and favor raising the minimum wage. They say they can make a difference and intend to try hard to do so.[58]

Nevertheless, the struggle against the privatization of public responsibilities is an uphill battle. This battle intensifies in third-world-south countries where economic constraints on governments create a particular crisis. Women in these regions are at risk in a number of ways. As the debt structure in africa is renegotiated by the IMF and World Bank, women must take up the slack left by nonexistent or severely limited government subsidies and programs. They work longer hours trying to supplement meager diets. They search for herbs instead of seeking medical help, which is unavailable.[59] They must creatively try to make do with scant resources.

Eastern europe since 1989 poses a particularly difficult situation for women. Much of communist statism has been replaced with privatized markets, and the results for women are quite mixed. Statist communism, which had its own form of statist feminism, provided day-care, soup kitchens and canteens at work, maternity leave, and other services that allowed women to do wage labor and maintain families at the same time. Now, capitalist markets displace women workers and eliminate these networks of support. As a result, large numbers of women are unemployed and state supports are gone. Many of these women are newly poor and desolate.

Although statist communism was no panacea for women, the new so-called 'democracies' have created a special kind of poverty for women; new consumer goods are everywhere to be seen while unemployed women have no money to spend.[60] Most women in poland, russia, the former yugoslavia, and other eastern european nations do not want to go back to old-style communist statism—with its tripled burdens of job, domestic labor, and long consumer lines but neither do they want to be forced into unemployment and privatized domesticity.

Egyptian feminists have long debated the role of the state in creating equality for women. With structural adjustment advised by the IMF and World Bank, Anwar Sadat oversaw the state employment of women and developed the social services necessary for this to happen. However, many of these services have been jeopardized by increasing privatization due to transnational capital.[61]

Nation-state support of women's equality is almost always double-edged. In the last decades of the twentieth century, feminism on behalf of the nation-state has embodied the tension between traditional familial patriarchy and transnational capitalist forms. In part, statist-feminism intervenes on behalf of modernizing male privilege. However, it also frees women from former patriarchal-racial structures that no longer assist changing economies. Today, there is less statist feminism to be found in the downsized transnation-state of global capital. Privatization has displaced claims for equality—be it economic, racial, or sexual.

Meanwhile, in subsaharan africa, where large parts of the continent have been written off by the banks and culture industries, tens of thousands of grassroots groups, led by women, are organizing to end hunger with new alternative farming methods, and to protect the environment from further onslaughts of global capital.[62] They demand solutions to their problems and are no longer waiting for first-world governments to take notice.

Women around the globe, across extraordinary differences, are affected by excessive poverty and the commercial exploitation of their sex. The 'real' vulnerabilities of women and girls provide an incentive to look beyond statist feminisms and transnational privatization. Dialogues among women moving in this direction were started at the women's conference in Beijing.

From Beijing to Transnational Publics

Beijing was the fourth in a series of U.N.-sponsored world conferences on women, the first of which was held in 1975, about the time that transnational capital solidified its global web.[63]

The Beijing conference provides a bookmark of sorts, noting the first time a global women's and girls' movement was pictured on the world stage by the mainstream news media. Of course, this presentation is not uncomplicated and raises an important question: Is this public viewing of women and girls simply a global fantasy that suits global capital, or are these feminist voices a significant challenge to the imaginary 'global village'? Beijing represents a bit of both: an adversarial moment that can and cannot be simply mainstreamed.

Beijing acts as a metaphor for the discrimination and exploitation of women and girls across the globe by the same cyber-media complex that is partially responsible for this condition. CNN, the *New York Times,* the net, and e-mail each played a different role in broadcasting and disseminating information about women's poverty, illiteracy, and health care needs.[64] But the very same technologies that make non mainstream discourse possible on e-mail and the net are also at the core of the information industries that exploit women and girls in both new and old ways.

The Beijing conference itself was more diverse than its CNN and *New York Times* presentation. Rather than one global women's movement, there are many women's movements across the globe. Keen differences of culture, economic class, race, and religion create almost insurmountable barriers. At the same time, sexual discrimination creates similarities that allow women to connect across differences of culture, region, and religion, even if just barely.

The official document of the conference, the *Platform for Action,* reveals high levels of difficult compromise among the women attending. It symbolizes a moment of deliberative dialogue and unity among women across the globe and, like any statement of compromise, it mutes the conflicts. The *Platform* demands that governments live up to their promises of sexual equality, and thus becomes an important device for post-Beijing feminist dialogue. A remaining challenge is to mobilize beyond Beijing's mainstream origins and articulate global visions critical of the excesses of transnational capital and its racialized patriarchal forms of exploitation and oppression.

First, let us examine the multiple and different interests present at the conference. The politics at Beijing ran the gamut: from U.N.-sponsored initiatives, to Islamic feminist readings of the Koran, to lesbian feminist gay rights actions, to equal rights discourse, and so on. As a result, multiple cultural and political discourses define the parameters of the *Platform.* Women are viewed as crucial to economic development. Sexual violence is highlighted as a major blight on women's and girl's lives. However, individualist and collectivist visions of these issues compete for space.

Language itself was a terrain of contestation. Words like "gender" were initially bracketed for being too suggestive of feminist and gay politics. But a feminist viewpoint prevailed: we "see the world through women's eyes."[65] The *Platform* strongly demands the elimination of all forms of discrimination—social, economic, and legal—against women, including any infringement on the right to freely choose the number and spacing of their children.[66] In this case, abortion is not clearly articulated as a right, but is recognized as a threat to women's reproductive health when unsafe.

Equal rights discourse underlies the discussions of poverty and violence against women. The specificity of women's rights requires us to rewrite universal rights discourse.[67] The right not to be poor and to be free of sexual violence need to be conceived as fundamental human rights. Given the feminization of poverty, women must have access to productive resources. Then, women's rights—to food or a job—are more generally connected to the universality of human rights and not consigned to a 'special' status.

Gertrude Mongella argues that although one global agenda is needed, it must recognize "that societies will be different, but built equally on the visions of men and women."[68] Women will play a key role in democratizing their societies by advancing their particular needs. As women become educated and free of violence, they will advance their countries along with themselves. In this scenario, women's advancement is viewed as crucial to economic and social development. "Women's knowledge and achievements help everyone. Women are concerned with the basic needs of society, with the creation of life and the preservation of the environment."[69] To improve women's lot—to eliminate illiteracy and malnutrition—is to improve the country as a whole.

In this view, the importance of women derives from their gendered role as mother of the nation; their significance stems from how they can improve the nation. Hillary Clinton fully rearticulated this position at Beijing and again while speaking in Belfast in 1997: "When women are empowered to make the most of their own potential, then their families will thrive. And when families thrive, communities and nations thrive as well."[70] But what does this actually, tangibly, mean for women in this time of transnational capital dominance?

This development approach may simply reclaim women's labor for the culture industries of global capital. Development discourse reproduces aspects of patriarchy and women's secondary status while modernizing the forms in which they occur. Given these shortcomings, however, the loosening of traditional patriarchal forms can still be liberating for women, even when sexual equality is far from sight.

The *Platform* can also be used as a critical lens on the development of transnational capital by naming women's global poverty and renewing the call for government action on behalf of women's rights. The embrace of equality-oriented governments at the Beijing conference is a first—though inadequate—step in combating the predominant discourse of privatization of governments across the globe. Today, the demand for affirmative governmental action on behalf of women is a radical request. The next step, of course, is to rethink how one can REALLY make this happen.

Even Mongella, the United Nations' official spokesperson, says that a commitment to action must be coupled with a commitment of resources. Governments must make themselves "accountable to the world's women."[71] But what does it really mean in today's world to ask the government for anything? As governments are asked to create equality for women, we must reckon with the 'real' ability of debt-ridden countries to stand against the pressures of transnational capital, as well as the embedded corruption of first-world transnation-states. Women must demand much of governments, but we cannot depend on the ones that presently exist.

The *Platform* calls for national mechanisms to assure women's involvement at the governmental level. This demand must go head-to-head with the requisites of transnational capital and its telecommunications empire. Otherwise, the rights discourse of Beijing will simply be absorbed into the rhetoric of consumer capitalism. Instead, a liberatory democracy inclusive of women must be imaged.[72] Post-1989 global politics makes this more urgent than ever.

Margarita Pisano, a chilean 'autonomous' feminist, rejects what she sees as the patriarchal feminism of Beijing, where English was the chosen language and the World Bank and the United Nations were sponsors. Virginia Vargas, another chilean feminist and a delegate to the conference, argues in response that both globalization and the conference create new possibilities for women. For Vargas, Beijing is not a feminist utopia, but a "multiple strategy," and a radicalism that rejects the possibility of "negotiating reforms is nothing more than fundamentalism" in a different guise.[73]

Beijing speaks of "women everywhere" and the interests of "all humanity."[74] The human rights of women and girls are integral and indivisible with the needs of the globe. But this framing of rights discourse means that there is no explicit mention of global patriarchy in the *Platform*. The demand for the prevention and elimination of all forms of violence against women and girls does not name men as the perpetrators.[75] Although men and women are described as living in different worlds—with women living in 'unspeakable poverty'—global capital, as such, is not named. Instead, shared partnerships of power and responsibility, between men and women at home, are envisioned. These relationships are a matter of human rights; they are conditions for social justice. The universality, indivisibility, and interrelatedness of human rights, once again, constructs the contours of women's rights.[76]

In this reading, women's rights require access to family planning, global immunization against childhood diseases, severe penalties for pre- and postnatal female infanticide, the elimination of traditional practices of female genital mutilation, and an end to illiteracy. These rights require activist, affirmative governments acting on behalf of women and girls.[77] Transnational capital, the cyber-media complex, and patriarchal divisions of labor and family, however, go unnamed.

The *Platform* has much to say about violence against women. It focuses on the responsibilities of government to condemn and take action to eliminate violence against women as an integral part of creating world peace. Violence against women and girls exists in all regions, classes, and cultures. It is "a major concern everywhere" and a main "matter of health and human rights."[78]

This indictment of violence had been a long time evolving from earlier human rights conferences in Vienna and Cairo.[79] Violence extends beyond domestic conflict, to sati, female genital mutilation, prostitution, infanticide, abuse of women in detention, rape as a war tactic, and so on.[80] The indictment locates violence against women as a human rights violation and radicalizes this discourse to extend beyond its traditional masculinist domains. In this frame, violence against women does not simply affect women, it degrades the public health. Public attention to violence against women reorients the unstated masculinism of human rights discourse to a more inclusive reading.

Approximately 100 to 130 million girls and women worldwide have undergone female genital mutilation (FGM)—the cutting off of part of the clitoris and/or part of the external genitalia. This practice endangers the health and welfare of girls, who are given no choice in the matter.[81] The women at Beijing saw FGM as a public health issue and demanded a different view of girls' rights.

The violence in sex trafficking was also highlighted and criticized at Beijing. An estimated 30 million women and girls have been forced into prostitution since the early 1970s. They face sexual slavery, debt-bondage, daily violence, and physical abuse. Young girls have become increasingly popular in the sex trade because it is assumed they are less likely to be infected with the AIDS virus.[82]

In addition to demanding freedom from violence, the *Platform* also highlights women's need to control their own bodies. A woman is not merely "a reproductive machine, but is a sexual being with rights."[83] She has the right to control when and if she bears a child. Her bodily self-determination is seen as a part of her right to gender equality. In this reading, women's human rights include control over their sexual and reproductive health, free of coercion, discrimination, and violence.

Beijing symbolically establishes reproductive and sexual self-determination as a basic health need and human right for women. The *Platform* reaffirms the right of all women to control all aspects of their health—especially fertility—as essential to their empowerment. It also requires that motherhood, parenting, and the role of women in procreation must not be a basis for discrimination or restrict the full participation of women in society.[84]

Governments are expected to take an active role here, too. Reproductive rights require the expansion and improvement of family-planning services. Prevention of unwanted pregnancies must be given high priority in order to limit the need for abortion. Unsafe abortions are named as a major public health concern. Of course, simply stating these commitments is not sufficient when abortion remains illegal in many countries, especially in south america and africa, and when abortion services are being severely curtailed even where they are legal.

In order to significantly increase women's access to quality health care, reproductive health resources must be made more available. Such a health policy demands an assault against the privatized commitments of transnational capital, its destruction of the environment, and the greed of the medical insurance industries. Little is said about these issues in the *Platform*.

Access to reproductive health envisions publics and communities that enable freedom to 'really' choose. In order to 'really' freely choose, one must have access to information and freedom from sexual violence. One must live in a society that values women and girls over profits and commercialism. This, of course, puts women head-to-head with the demands of transnational capital and its racialized patriarchal consumer cultures. The U.N.-sponsored Beijing conference sidestepped these dilemmas.

Sexual Rights and Transnational Democracy

By specifying the particular bodily needs of women, reproductive and sexual rights require us to form a more inclusive notion of public/community life. The public is then explicitly made up of men *and* women. Bodily integrity and sexual freedom can lead us to *re*form and mobilize a nonpatriarchal discourse of rights that challenges transnational capital. These 'imaginings' of a democratic globe for women and girls, and therefore humanity, initiate countervoices to the mainstream cyber-media complex.

Although the discourse of sexual rights was still in its infancy at Beijing, Rosalind Petchesky thinks that "an affirmative approach to sexual rights" can deploy a wide-ranging set of enabling conditions. She believes that discussions about fertility and motherhood sometimes ambiguously stand in for "assertive declarations of sexual freedom in order for women themselves to negotiate different orientations toward the body."[85]

Language matters because we see and hope through it. The language of Beijing might just have given voice to a revolutionary process that is not tied to the constraints of the U.N. conference. Whether in bosnia or rwanda, the United Nations—looking more helpless than helpful with little muscle to flex—is an unlikely ally in the struggle against global capital. But women across the globe may just go ahead and build their own coalitions.

New talk about what democracy means for women and girls opens up refreshingly new possibilities for deliberation. Women's and girls' bodies determine democracy: free from violence and sexual abuse, free from malnutrition and environmental degradation, free to plan their families, free to not have families, free to choose their sexual lives and preferences.

This will require a new relationship between women and the people they love, AND a public-regarding local entity to ensure that sexual and racial equality prevails over transnational capital. Localized controls on the cyber-media complex and its telecommunications networks will allow "non-territorial principles of solidarity"[86] that nurture nonpatriarchal/racialized constructions of identity to flourish.

Such new imaginings will be needed to replace the hyperreal of consumer capital. Carolyn Merchant points in the right direction when she calls for a respect for nature's autonomy and chaos, protection of the environment, and a limit to building so that open space remains. She argues that each person must be recognized as a part of the "earth's household."[87] In this imaginary, the public/private divide does not hold in its traditional form, not because it has merged, but because it is disarranged. While living in the globe locally, the local is *also* individually specified—in the body of a girl or woman wishing to not be pregnant against her will, or to attend school instead of working in the factory, or to be truly loved by another.

Most women (and many men) want a more liberatory globe. Women in japan, outraged by the rape of a young girl by an american serviceman in Okinawa, speak of the "common desire" women share for peace in the twenty-first century. They demand an end to the sexual crimes and sexual slavery perpetrated by the militaries of the world.[88] They hope for a new kind of policing of masculinist militarism.

Many women in Islamic societies want "more equality under secular law" and a more active role in Islamic religious life. They wish to claim their democratic rights as Muslim women, whether religious or secular.[89] Israeli and palestinian women demand peace as part of democracy. A new women's movement in northern ireland hopes to sit at the irish bargaining table to democratize the process and create what they see as a different public accountability.

Many women across the globe are building dialogues that contribute to a deliberative public discourse that deploys public-mindedness in the fight against violence, hunger, poverty, the destruction of the environment, and sexual/racial oppression. Some women see transnational capitalist patriarchy and its consumerist culture as the 'real' culprit of these evils, while others see different variations of this theme.

In order to build transnational democratic discussions and actions, women will have to deliberate carefully and continually across political, cultural, and economic differences. Such dialogue—which both mutes and invites conflict—can build a transnational public of women's and girls' voices that creates the very same liberatory democratic process it imagines. Cyberspace holds out new promise for these processes to take shape.

Net Feminism and Virtual Sisterhoods

Feminism on the net needs to be recognized and nourished. At the same time, demands for access to the new information technologies must become a basic commitment of these feminist expressions. Although many sites on the net are dominated by pornography, there are significant countervoices demanding women's rights and an end to women's exploitation. The net reflects society and the privileges of power much as they exist in the real world AND creates countless possibilities for critiquing them. Yet, we must also keep in mind that approximately 100 million children, including at *least* 60 million girls, are without access to primary schooling, and that more than two-thirds of the world's illiterate are women.[90]

I do not mean to idealize or fantasize the REAL power-effects of cyberdialogue today. The first time my twelve-year-old daughter and I cybersearched the phrase 'girl's rights' we came up with over twelve thousand sites. Almost all of the first two hundred listings we looked at were porn: wet pussy, kinky sex, teen fucking, horny girls, nude girls, amazing teen cocksuckers, ass pussy, and so on. 'Girls' clearly means sex/porn in virtual space. 'Girl's rights' has yet to be created in VR (virtual reality).

Nevertheless, cyberspace and its information technologies can be used as a participatory location for dialogue by women attempting to speak across the divides of time, space, and geography. Webzines, internet listserves, e-mail networks, and activist newsgroups create new dialogic spaces, which in turn create new collectivities and public spaces for building coalitions.

On the net, feminists send and receive information via e-mail and listserves as a form of empowerment.[91] These women use cybertechnologies as a resource for fighting against poverty and war and creating access to nonmainstream news about women's health.

Disparate political venues exist for cyberfeminists. Mainstream western women's/feminist groups predominate. They have more access to the technologies and are better funded than third-world-south feminist voices. English remains the reigning language. Despite these serious limitations, feminisms on the net should be recognized for their significant political potential—NOT as a replacement for political activism, but as a tool to help organize women around the globe.

Net feminisms are a different kind of politics, an additional form of interaction and dialogue.[92] They are not meant to stand in for collective expressions of real 'bodied' women, but rather to enhance these connections when onsite action and deliberation are impossible. As mainstream news becomes more and more concentrated and controlled, e-mail and listserves become alternative sources of information upon which to build a counterpolitics.

The National Organization for Women (NOW) in the united states has a website for its Women-Friendly Workplace Campaign. The site has drawn people from sixteen countries interested in sharing and learning about sex discrimination and harassment on the job. People share personal stories and exchange ideas about possible actions.[93]

Bat Shalom is a feminist center committed to peace and social justice. It e-mails men and women across the globe to publicize its message "that we can no longer ignore the rights of Palestinians who live in the city, and that we cannot reach peace until both Israelis and Palestinians will learn to live with each other and compromise."[94] Bat Shalom works "toward a democratic and pluralistic society in Israel, where women will be of more influence." The Jerusalem Center for Women, the palestinian counterpart of Bat Shalom, was founded in 1994. Together they form the Jerusalem Link—israeli and palestinian women working for peace.

Young girls and teens can find a friendly guide to the internet that lists sites in which girls (or grrrls) can find information and initiate dialogues with others who have similar concerns related to their particular problems as teens.[95]

The Virtual Sisterhood (VS) home page welcomes women in nine languages: chinese, german, english, spanish, french, hebrew, italian, japanese, and russian. VS wishes "to create and facilitate a global network of women committed to enhancing their own and other women's activism through effective use of electronic communications." VS is particularly concerned to include and empower "women of color, immigrant and refugee women, low-income women, lesbians, women from the Global South, older women, young women, women with disabilities, rural women and women from other communities, which have traditionally had little or no access to or control of electronic communications technology." The priority is to use electronic information resources to enhance social justice for ALL women.[96]

Geekgirl is a cyberzine designed by Rosie X in 1995. According to Amelia DeLoach *geekgirl* expressed a feminist stance opposed to the internet "boy's club." But grrrls on the web don't have a singular purpose. Rosie X thinks that the idea of a movement homogenizes women too much, as though all women have the same needs, wants, and desires. However, De-Loach notes that it was impotent rage at the media and pop culture that originated the grrrl movement. The movement is diffuse, but very powerful.[97]

Cyberfeminist Sadie Plant argues in *geekgirl,* that women must embrace their connection to the machines of cyberspace. Women can find new autonomy in these technologies.[98] Another cyberfeminist, Rosi Braidotti at the University of Utrecht, images the body as a 'metaphor' for power. She urges women to disengage from the phallus and liberate themselves from the confines of the body.[99]

JUST WATCH is an internet and e-mail project originating from Zurich, Switzerland, that addresses the question of access to and alternative use of the electronic media by women from africa, south america, and asia. JUST WATCH focuses on the construction and mobilization of social divisions based on gender and race and the way they are used by a globalizing politics of mass communication to exclude minorities, migrants, and marginalized women. According to founding member Ursula Biemann, JUST WATCH is organized entirely via e-mail. "The virtual sisterhood network really works," she says. E-mail has "opened up the scope of activities tremendously . . . it is how we heard about the media platform in Beijing . . . it is how we connected to the media union women to collaborate." These networks were used to develop an international symposium in Zurich in September 1997 where theorists and media activists/producers came together in 'real space' to overcome the isolation in their own countries and talk about strategies for change.[100]

The Urban Justice Center in New York City uses many women's listserves to distribute information and call for petition signatures against many of the new welfare/workfare regulations. In August 1997, a Workfare Pledge of Resistance was circulated through feminist e-mail networks that called for an "end to workfare" and "the creation of living-wage jobs for all."

Most western feminist organizations are online today. The Global Fund for Women fights for women's human rights—against domestic violence and the trafficking of women, and for economic justice and women's literacy across the globe. There are feminist sites originating in england, sweden, switzerland, canada, and other countries.[101] There are sites featuring digital images of artwork from women as a kind of global exhibition format.[102]

FemiNet Korea promises an electronic space for women that challenges the male privilege of the information society. *Aviva,* a feminist zine, posts an information bulletin about workers' rights in bangladesh, brazil, burma, cambodia, and indonesia. It lists the names of women who are arrested in work actions and calls for the release of imprisoned women in turkey and detained women in nigeria and pakistan.[103]

Women in russia and in other postcommunist states use the net to let the rest of the world's women know what is happening to them in their new economies. These women try to build new bridges across the globe.[104] Women antiwar activists in Belgrade continuously used e-mail to counter their isolation during the war.

These cyberdialogues exist between the cracks of mainstream news reporting and people's everyday lives. Such communication allows for diasporic publics to connect with one another and initiates new alliances with people 'outside' one's immediate geographical region. These disparate and dispersed communications can be used to build structures for change and mobilize struggles for peace, equality, and a healthy environment.

However, getting information is not the same thing as acting on it, just like virtual reality is not the same thing as bodily reality. Thinking, knowing, and acting are distinct parts of a process that require different strategies. If cyberspace can be used to enhance and expand the connections among these realms—beyond the limits of bodies and local geographies—a politics demanding access to information technologies becomes central to the struggle against transnational capital.

The globe must be deprivatized and the locales in which we live re-civilized. Coalitions must be built to make the globe a habitable home. Cybertechnologies can subversively assist this process by allowing new modes of communication across the indecent racial/patriarchal divides. As women demand access to cyberspace—both to move beyond the confines of the body's geography AND to enhance the freedom of bodies—a different world is imagined. Such IMAGINATION is subversively hopeful because it indicts the REAL.

notes

Notes to the Introduction

1. Robert D. Kaplan, "Was Democracy Just a Moment?" *Atlantic Monthly,* vol. 280, no. 6 (December 1997): 71.

2. Zillah Eisenstein, ed., *Capitalist Patriarchy and the Case for Socialist Feminism* (New York: Monthly Preview Press, 1979).

3. Zillah Eisenstein, *The Color of Gender* (Berkeley: University of California Press, 1994); and *HATREDS, Racialized and Sexualized Conflicts of the Twenty-First Century* (New York: Routledge, 1996).

4. Karl Marx and Friedrich Engels, *The Communist Manifesto* (Chicago: Gateway Press, 1954).

Notes to Chapter 1

1. For a similar methodology applied to the body, see the introduction to Elizabeth Grosz and Elspeth Probyn, eds., *Sexy Bodies* (New York: Routledge, 1995), pp. ix–xi.

2. I am indebted to Salman Rushdie for my use of this metaphor. See his delightful book, *The Wizard of Oz* (Worcester: British Film Institute, 1992).

3. Susan Faludi, "Swedish Sojourn," *Ms. Magazine,* vol. 6, no. 5 (March–April 1996): 64–71.

4. I am rephrasing C. W. Mills's notion of a military-industrial complex. See his *The Power Elite* (New York: Oxford University Press, 1959).

5. Ellen Meiksins Wood, "Issues of Class and Culture: An Interview with Aijaz Ahmad," *Monthly Review,* vol. 48, no. 5 (October 1996): 14.

6. Randy Albelda, Nancy Folbre, and the Center for Popular Economics, *The War on the Poor* (New York: New Press, 1996), p. 76.

7. As quoted in Bob Herbert, "A Loss of Nerve," *New York Times,* January 27, 1997, p. A17.

8. William Julius Wilson, *When Work Disappears: The World of the New Urban Poor* (New York: Alfred A. Knopf, 1996).

9. Mark Dery, *Escape Velocity, Cyberculture at the End of the Century* (New York: Grove Press, 1996), p. 14.

10. Mark Lewyn, "Electric Word," *WIRED* 4.10 (October 1996) 41.

11. Jean Baudrillard, *Simulations*, trans. Paul Foss, Paul Patton, and Philip Beitchman (New York: Semiotext[e], 1983), p. 97.

12. Jean Baudrillard, *The Mirror of Production*, trans. Mark Poster (St. Louis: Telos Press, 1975), p. 7.

13. Mark Poster, "Critical Theory and Technoculture: Habermas and Baudrillard," in Douglas Kellner, ed., *Baudrillard: A Critical Reader* (Oxford: Blackwell, 1994), pp. 77, 81.

14. Steven Best, "The Commodification of Reality and the Reality of Commodification: Baudrillard, Debord, and Postmodern Theory," in Kellner, ed., *Baudrillard,* p. 52.

15. Douglas Kellner, "Introduction: Jean Baudrillard in the Fin-de-Millennium", in Kellner, ed., *Baudrillard,* p. 1.

16. Baudrillard, *Simulations,* p. 96.

17. Mark Poster, editor's introduction to *Jean Baudrillard: Selected Writings* (Stanford: Stanford University Press, 1988), p. 6.

18. Baudrillard, Simulations, pp. 2, 5.

19. Ibid., pp. 147, 152, 141, 16.

20. Ibid., p. 47.

21. Howard Rheingold, *The Virtual Community* (New York: Harper-Perennial, 1993), p. 299.

22. Jean Baudrillard, *The Gulf War Did Not Take Place*, trans. Paul Patton (Bloomington: Indiana University Press, 1995), p. 8.

23. Baudrillard, *Mirror of Production,* p. 128.

24. Baudrillard, *The Gulf War Did Not Take Place,* p. 27.

25. Baudrillard, *Simulations,* p. 25.

26. Ada Louise Huxtable, "Living with the Fake and Liking It," *New York Times,* March 30, 1997, p. H1.

27. Nicholas Negroponte, *Being Digital* (New York: Vintage, 1995), p. 116.

28. Elizabeth Reid, "Virtual Worlds: Culture and Imagination," in Steven Jones, ed., *Cybersociety* (Newbury Park, Calif.: Sage Publications, 1995), p. 166.

29. Jean Baudrillard, *For Critique of the Political Economy of the Sign*, trans. Charles Levin (St. Louis: Telos Press, 1981), pp. 164, 165.

30. Ibid., pp. 165, 166.

31. Paul Patton, introduction to Baudrillard, *The Gulf War Did Not Take Place*, p. 7.

32. Ibid., p. 9.

33. Baudrillard, *Mirror of Production*, pp. 127, 122.

34. Christopher Norris, *Uncritical Theory: Postmodernism, Intellectuals, and the Gulf War* (Amherst: University of Massachusetts Press, 1992), pp. 11–14. See also Jeffrey Walsh, ed., *The Gulf War Did Not Happen*, "Popular Cultural Studies," 7 (Aldershot, England: Arena, 1995).

35. For an extremely interesting set of discussions about the 'real' of race, see Toni Morrison and Claudia Brodsky Lacour, eds., *Birth of a Nation'hood: Gaze, Script, and Spectacle in the O. J. Simpson Case* (New York: Pantheon, 1997).

36. Baudrillard, *The Gulf War Did Not Take Place*, p. 59.

37. Ibid., p. 84.

38. Baudrillard, *Political Economy of the Sign*, pp. 169, 172.

39. Ibid., pp. 169–77.

40. "Telecommunications," *The Economist*, October 23, 1993, p. 5.

41. *Universal Service and the Information Superhighway*, Benton Foundation Communications Policy Briefing 1, 1994. Available from Benton Foundation, 1634 Eye Street NW, Washington, D.C. 20006.

42. For related discussions see Bruce Robbins, ed., *The Phantom Public Sphere* (Minneapolis: University of Minnesota Press, 1993).

43. Jürgen Habermas, *The Structural Transformation of the Public Sphere* (Cambridge: MIT Press, 1989).

44. Walter Lippmann, *The Phantom Public* (New York: Harcourt, Brace, 1925).

45. As cited in Daniel Yankelovich, "Restoring the Public Trust," *Mother Jones*, vol. 20, no. 6 (November–December, 1995): 30.

46. Ray Oldenburg, *The Great Good Place* (New York: Paragon, 1989).

47. Susan Williams, "Globalization, Privatization and a Feminist Public," paper presented at the Feminism and Globalization Conference, University of Indiana Law School, March 22, 1996, published in *Indiana Journal of Global Legal Studies*, vol. 4, no. 1 (fall 1996): 101.

48. Cited in Elizabeth Kolbert and Adam Clymer, "The Politics of Layoffs: In Search of a Message," *New York Times*, March 8, 1996, p. A1.

49. Leo Panitch, ed., *Are There Alternatives? Socialist Register '96* (New York: Monthly Review Press, 1996).

50. George Soros, "The Capitalist Threat," *Atlantic Monthly*, vol. 279, no. 2 (February 1997): 48.

51. Gregory S. Alexander and Grazyna Skapska, *A Fourth Way?* (New York: Routledge, 1994).

52. Saskia Sassen, "Whose City Is It? Globalization and the Formation of New Claims," *Public Culture*, vol. 8, no. 2 (winter 1996): 215.

53. See "Setting the Record Straight/The Real Disney in Burma, Haiti, Indonesia and China," *National Labor Coalition Newsletter,* January 17, 1997. Available from the Educational Fund in Support of Workers and Human Rights in Central America, 275 7th Ave., New York, N.Y., 10011.

54. John Keane, "On Tools and Language: Habermas on Work and Interaction," *New German Critique*, no. 6 (summer 1975): 84–85. See also Peter Hohendahl, "Jürgen Habermas: The Public Sphere (1964)," *New German Critique*, no. 3 (fall 1974): 45–55.

55. Benjamin Barber, *Jihad vs. McWorld* (New York: Random House, 1995), p. 77.

56. Michael Sandel, "American's Search for a New Public Philosophy," *Atlantic Monthly*, vol. 277, no. 3 (March 1996): 57–74. See also

Leonard Silk and Mark Silk, *Making Capitalism Work* (New York: New York University Press, 1996).

57. Jean Cohen and Andrew Arato, *Civil Society and Political Theory* (Cambridge: MIT Press, 1992); and Ronald Beiner, ed., *Theorizing Citizenship* (Albany: State University of New York Press, 1995).

58. Michael Kelly, "Glasshouse Conventions," *New Yorker*, September 9, 1996, pp. 34–40.

59. Paul Goldberger, "The Store Strikes Back," *New York Times Magazine*, April 6, 1997, pp. 45–49.

60. Barber, *Jihad vs. McWorld*, p. 286.

61. Stuart Hall, "Ethnicity, Identity and Difference" *Radical America*, vol. 23, no. 4 (October–December 1989): 9–20.

62. Lippmann, *The Phantom Public*, pp. 77, 155, 199.

63. Alex Dupuy, "The New World Order and Social Change in the Americas: Ten Theses," *Radical America*, vol. 25, no. 4 (October–December, 1991): 7–24.

64. Alexander and Skapska, introduction to *A Fourth Way?* p. xi.

65. Michael Ignatieff, "The Myth of Citizenship," in Beiner, ed., *Theorizing Citizenship*, p. 76.

66. Anthony Giddens, *The Consequences of Modernity* (Stanford: Stanford University Press, 1990), pp. 125, 149.

67. See Mark Juergensmeyer, *The New Cold War?* (Berkeley: University of California Press, 1993), for related discussions.

68. Partha Chatterjee, *The Nation and Its Fragments* (Princeton: Princeton University Press, 1993), pp. 220–239.

69. Joseph Romm and Charles Curtis, "Mideast Oil Forever?" *Atlantic Monthly*, vol. 277, no. 4 (April 1996): 57, 62.

70. Carl Malamud, "Building a Park on RSA," *WIRED* 4.10 (October 1996): 134.

71. Paulina Borsook, "CyberSelfish," *Mother Jones*, vol. 21, no. 4 (July–August 1996): 55.

72. Anthony DePalma, "Protesters Take to Streets to Defend Canada's Safety Net," *New York Times*, October 26, 1996, p. A3.

73. Peter T. Kilborn, "Shrinking Safety Net Cradles Hearts and Hopes of Children," *New York Times*, November 30, 1996, p. A1.

74. Jason DeParle, "Cutting Welfare Rolls But Raising Questions," *New York Times*, May 7, 1997, p. A1.

75. Barbara Crossette, "Citizenship Is a Malleable Concept," *New York Times*, August 18, 1996, p. E3.

76. Steven Erlanger, "If Right Is Center, Where is Left?" *New York Times*, August 18, 1996, p. E1.

77. Peg Whitaker, "The Tower of Infobabel: Cyberspace as Alternative Universe," in Panitch, ed., *Are There Alternatives?* p. 178.

78. John Kennedy, "Colin Wants You," *George*, May 1997, pp. 78–82.

79. Edward Soja, *Postmodern Geographies* (London: Verso, 1989), p. 80.

80. Herbert Schiller, *Information Inequality* (New York: Routledge, 1996).

81. James Brook and Iain A. Boal, eds., *Resisting the Virtual Life* (San Francisco: City Lights, 1995), p. ix.

82. Ibid., p. xii.

83. Malcolm Howard, "No Freedom of Information," *WIRED* 5.04 (April, 1997): 90.

84. Jon Katz, "Netizen: Birth of a Digital Nation," *WIRED*, 5.04 (April, 1997): 50.

85. Jon Katz, *Virtuous Reality* (New York: Random House, 1997), p. xxi.

86. Quoted in Thomas A. Bass, "The Future of Money: Interview with Walter Wriston," *WIRED* 4.10 (October 1996): 202.

87. David S. Bennahum, "The Internet Revolution," *WIRED* 5.04 (April 1997): 172.

88. Geremie R. Barme and Sang Ye, "The Great Frewall of China," *WIRED* 5.06 (June 1997): 143, 176.

89. Ibid., p. 143.

90. John Carlin, "Netizen: Farewell to Arms," *WIRED* 5.05 (May 1997): 220, 52.

91. Mark Landler, "The Coming Phone War between City and Country," *New York Times*, May 12, 1997, p. D7.

92. Interview with Umberto Eco by Lee Marshall, "The World According to Eco," *WIRED* 5.03 (March 1997): 146, 147.

93. Jean-François Lyotard, *The Postmodern Condition: A Report on Knowledge* (Minneapolis: University of Minnesota Press, 1989), p. 67.

Notes to Chapter 2

1. Fredric Jameson, *Postmodernism, or, The Cultural Logic of Late Capitalism* (Durham: Duke University Press, 1995), p. 68.

2. There is a massive literature dealing with the creation of mass culture. A few of the best discussions are Stuart Ewen, *All Consuming Images* (New York: Basic Books, 1988) and his *Captains of Consciousness* (New York: Basic Books, 1976); Edward Herman and Noam Chomsky, *Manufacturing Consent* (New York: Pantheon, 1988); and Herbert Marcuse, *One Dimensional Man* (Boston: Beacon Press, 1964).

3. Jon Katz, *Virtuous Reality* (New York: Random House, 1997), p. 99.

4. Douglas Kellner, *Television and the Crisis of Democracy* (Boulder, Colo.: Westview, 1990), p. 12.

5. Mark Crispin Miller, "The Crushing Power of Big Publishing," *The Nation*, March 17, 1997, pp. 11–18.

6. Robert McChesney, "The Global Struggle for Democratic Communication," *Monthly Review*, vol. 48, no. 3 (July–August 1996): 3.

7. Mark Landler, "Westinghouse to Acquire 98 Radio Stations," *New York Times*, September 20, 1997, p. D1.

8. See Ben Bagdikian, *The Media Monopoly* (Boston: Beacon Press, 1983); Mark Crispin Miller, *Boxed In* (Evanston, Ill.: Northwestern University Press, 1988); and Neil Postman, *Amusing Ourselves to Death* (New York: Viking, 1985).

9. John Fiske, *Media Matters* (Minneapolis: University of Minnesota Press, 1994).

10. Michael Dawson and John Bellamy Foster, "Virtual Capitalism:

The Political Economy of the Information Highway," *Monthly Review,* vol. 48, no. 3 (July–August 1996): 47.

11. Robin Andersen, *Consumer Culture and TV Programming* (Boulder, Colo.: Westview, 1995), pp. 7, 9, 10. See also James B. Twitchell, *ADCULT USA: The Triumph of Advertising in American Culture* (New York: Columbia University Press, 1996).

12. Anderson, *Consumer Culture,* pp. 50, 96.

13. Mark Poster, ed., *Jean Baudrillard: Selected Writings* (Stanford: Stanford University Press, 1988), pp. 207, 211.

14. Umberto Eco, *Apocalypse Postponed,* ed. Robert Lumley (Bloomington: Indiana University Press, 1994), pp. 7, 17.

15. Thomas Bass, "The Future of Money; An Interview with Walter Wriston," *WIRED* 4.10 (October 1996): 201.

16. As quoted in Ed Vulliamy, "Middle Managers of Genocide," *The Nation,* June 10, 1996, p. 12.

17. Hamid Mowlana, George Gerbner, and Herbert I. Schiller, eds., *Triumph of the Image, The Media's War in the Persian Gulf—A Global Perspective* (Boulder, Colo.: Westview, 1992).

18. Henry Louis Gates, "The Naked Republic," *New Yorker,* August 25–September 1, 1997, p. 118.

19 Erik Barnouw and Patricia Zimmermann, eds., "The Flaherty: Four Decades in the Cause of Independent Cinema," *Wide Angle,* vol. 17, nos. 1–4 (1995).

20. For a similar discussion, see Katha Pollitt, "Thoroughly Modern Di," *The Nation,* September 29, 1997, p. 9. See also a series of articles in *The New Yorker,* September 15, 1997.

21. For an interesting discussion of the progressive possibilities of the talk show, see Jane M. Shattuc, *The Talking Cure, TV Talk Shows and Women* (New York: Routledge, 1997).

22. Mike A. Males, *The Scapegoat Generation* (Monroe, Me.: Common Courage Press, 1996), especially chaps. 2 and 9.

23. James Brooke, "All-American Defendant? Lawyer Works to Soften Image of Bombing Suspect," *New York Times,* June 2, 1996, p. A14.

24. Peter Edelman, "The Worst Thing Bill Clinton Has Done," *Atlantic Monthly,* vol. 279, no. 3 (March 1997): 43–58; David Ellwood, "Welfare Reform in Name Only," *New York Times,* July 22, 1996, p. A19; Bob Herbert, "The Mouths of Babes," *New York Times,* July 22, 1996, p. A19; and Katha Pollitt, "Just the Facts," *The Nation,* June 24, 1996, p. 9.

25. Kristin Luker, *Dubious Conceptions: The Politics of Teenage Pregnancy* (Cambridge: Harvard University Press, 1996), p. 1.

26. Frank Rich, "The Disney Trap," *New York Times,* August 5, 1995, p. A19.

27. Jean Baudrillard, *America,* trans. Chris Turner (London: Verso, 1988), pp. 27–29.

28. Ibid., pp. 95, 39, 40.

29. Hans Magnus Enzensberger, *The Consciousness Industry* (New York: Seabury Press, 1974).

30. Armand Mattelart, *Mapping World Communication: War, Progress, Culture,* trans. Susan Emanuel and James Cohen (Minneapolis, University of Minnesota Press, 1994), and his *Transnationals and the Third World: The Struggle for Culture,* trans. David Buxton (South Hadley, Mass.: Bergin and Garvey, 1983). See also Walter Benjamin, *Illuminations,* trans. Harry Zohn (New York: Schocken, 1969); and Susan Buck-Morss, *The Dialectics of Seeing* (Cambridge: MIT Press, 1989).

31. Holly Sklar, *Chaos or Community?* (Boston: South End Press, 1995).

32. Jeremy Rifkin, "Civil Society in the Information Age," *The Nation,* February 26, 1996, pp. 11–16. See also his *The End of Work* (New York: G. P. Putnam's Sons, 1995).

33. Joe McGinniss, *The Selling of the President* (New York: Trident Press, 1964), pp. 26, 27.

34. Daniel Boorstin, *The Image* (New York: Atheneum, 1961), pp. ix, 3, 5, 239.

35. Andersen, *Consumer Culture,* pp. 36, 43, 49.

36. Douglas Rushkoff, *Media Virus! Hidden Agendas in Popular Culture* (New York: Ballantine Books, 1994), p. 222.

37. Miller, *Boxed In*, p. 235.

38. Howard Rheingold, *Virtual Reality* (New York: Summit Books, 1991), p. 17.

39. James Fallows, *Breaking the News: How the Media Undermine American Democracy* (New York: Pantheon, 1996), pp. 6, 8.

40. Thomas de Zengotita, "Celebrity, Irony and You," *The Nation*, December 2, 1996, p. 15.

41. Pat Aufderheide, "The Media Monopolies Muscle In," *The Nation*, January 3–10, 1994, pp. 1–21.

42. Bill Mesler, "Hotline to the White House," *The Nation*, June 30, 1997, p. 20.

43. Bernard Weinraub, "It's a Small World, After All, Mr. Eisner," *New York Times*, August 7, 1995, p. D1.

44. Mark Crispin Miller, "Free the Media," *The Nation*, June 3, 1996, pp. 9–28.

45. Dan Kennedy, "Making Sense of Merger Mania," in Don Hazen and Larry Smith, eds., *Media and Democracy* (San Francisco: Institute for Alternative Journalism, 1996), p. 9. E-mail: alternet@alternet.org

46. See the conference report of the Telecommunications Act of 1996, Senate Report 104–230, 104th Congress, 2d Session. Available from U.S. Senate, Washington, D.C., 20510–3301.

47. Robert McChesney, "The Internet and the Future of Democracy," in Hazen and Smith, eds., *Media and Democracy*, pp. 24, 25.

48. Rheingold, *Virtual Community*, pp. 86, 89.

49. Frank Rich, "The Idiot Chip," *New York Times*, February 10, 1996, p. A23.

50. Edmund Andrews, "It's Confounded Change Calling Again, Honey," *New York Times*, December 26, 1993, p. E3.

51. Telecommunications Act of 1996, pp. 187–196.

52. See Zillah Eisenstein, *Feminism and Sexual Equality: Crisis in Liberal America* (New York: Monthly Review Press, 1984).

53. John D'Emilio and Estelle B. Freedman, *Intimate Matters: A History of Sexuality in America* (New York: Harper and Row, 1988).

54. John Markoff, "On-Line Service Blocks Access to Topics Called

Pornographic," *New York Times*, December 29, 1995, p. A1; Erik Ashok Meers, "New Technology, Old Rhetoric," *The Advocate*, March 19, 1996, pp. 23–24; and Laurence Tribe, "The Constitution in Cyberspace," *Humanist Review*, vol. 51, no. 5 (September–October 1991): 17–21.

55. Benjamin Barber, "From Disney World to Disney's World," *New York Times*, August 1, 1995, p. A15; and Maureen Dowd, "Mickey Mouse News," *New York Times*, August 3, 1995, p. A25.

56. Colleen Ballerino Cohen, Richard Wilk, and Beverly Stoeltje, eds., *Beauty Queens on the Global Stage* (New York: Routledge, 1996).

57. Masao Miyoshi, "A Borderless World? From Colonialism to Transnationalism and the Decline of the Nation State," *Critical Inquiry*, vol. 19, no. 4 (summer 1993): 728, 741.

58. Susan Buck-Morss, "Aesthetics and Anaesthetics: Walter Benjamin's Artwork Essay Reconsidered," *October*, no. 62 (fall 1992): 3–41.

59. Neoconservativism is a political stance, originating in the early 1970s, that attempts to redefine and reform the radical promise of liberal democracy away from the demands for equality. Neocons, also termed neoliberals, wish to emphasize the 'original' meaning of opportunity and individual freedom within liberal democratic discourse. See Zillah Eisenstein, *The Color of Gender* (Berkeley: University of California Press, 1994).

60. Jean Baudrillard, *For a Critique of the Political Economy of the Sign*, trans. Charles Levin (St. Louis: Telos Press, 1981); and Jean Baudrillard, *The Mirror of Production*, trans. Mark Poster (St. Louis: Telos Press, 1975).

61. Russell Baker, "Sex to the Rescue," *New York Times*, August 31, 1996, p. A21.

62. Elaine Sciolino, "As Clinton Gains with Women He Falls in Eyes of Many Men," *New York Times*, October 6, 1996, p. A1.

63. Neil MacFarquhar, "What's a Soccer Mom Anyway?" *New York Times*, October 20, 1996, p. E1.

64. Steven Stark, "Gap Politics," *Atlantic Monthly*, vol. 278, no. 1 (July 1996): 71–80.

65. Taken from a poll reported in *Good Housekeeping*, vol. 223, no. 3 (September 1996): 14.

66. Gail Collins, "Wooing the Women," *New York Times Magazine*, July 28, 1996, pp. 32–35.

67. Elinor Burkett, "In the Land of Conservative Women," *Atlantic Monthly*, vol. 278, no. 3 (September 1996): 29.

68. According to Nat Hentoff ("Bill Clinton's Judges," *Village Voice*, October 29, 1996, p. 25), judges appointed by Clinton have written liberal decisions 35 percent of the time, whereas Jimmy Carter's did so 52 percent; Gerald Ford's 39 percent; and Richard Nixon's 37 percent.

69. Quoted in Frank Rich, "Dole's Pregnant Silence," *New York Times*, October 19, 1996, p. A23.

70. Roger Morris, *Partners in Power* (New York: Henry Holt, 1996); and Bob Woodward, *The Choice* (New York: Simon and Schuster, 1996).

71. Erica Jong, "Hillary's Husband Re-Elected!" *The Nation*, November 25, 1996, p. 14.

72. Todd S. Purdum, "Advisers See Bright Side to Criticism of First Lady," *New York Times*, August 25, 1996, p. A1. See also Eisenstein, *HATREDS*, chap. 5, for a full analysis of Hillary Clinton.

73. Maureen Dowd, "Plowshares into Pacifiers," *New York Times*, August 16, 1996, p. A27.

74. Sam Howe Verhovek, "With Abortion Scarcely Uttered, Its Opponents Are Feeling Angry," *New York Times*, August 15, 1996, p. A1.

75. Katherine Seelye, "Under Pressure, Dole Reconsiders Abortion Plank," *New York Times*, July 13, 1996, p. A1; and her "Moderates in G.O.P. Vow Fight On Platform Abortion Language," *New York Times*, August 7, 1996, p. A1.

76. Russell Baker, "In the Attic? Hillary?" *New York Times*, August 3, 1996, p. A19.

77. Adam Nagourney, "On Volatile Social and Cultural Issues, Silence," *New York Times*, October 9, 1996, p. A1.

78. For an interesting discussion about the conflicts surrounding

abortion in the Republican party, see Susan Faludi, "The G.O.P.'s Back Stairs," *New York Times*, August 18, 1996, p. E15.

79. Quoted in John Heilemann, "Netizen: Big Brother Bill," *Wired* 4.10 (October 1996): 199.

80. Peter Kilborn and Sam Howe Verhovek, "Clinton's Welfare Shift Reflects New Democrat," *New York Times*, August 2, 1996, p. A1.Peter Kilborn and Sam Howe Verhovek, "Clinton's Welfare Shift Reflects New Democrat", *New York Times*, August 2, 1996, p. A1.

81. From the text of "President Clinton's Announcement on Welfare Legislation," *New York Times*, August 1, 1996, p. A24.

82. Robert Pear, "Clinton Says He Will Sign Welfare Bill to End U.S. Guarantee," *New York Times*, August 1, 1996, p. A22.

83. *Update*, no. 2 (June 1996), available from the Women's Committee of One Hundred, 750 First Street NE, Suite 700, Washington, D.C. 20002.

84. Alan Finder, "Welfare Clients Outnumber Jobs They Might Fill," *New York Times*, August 25, 1996, p. A1.

85. Randy Albelda, Nancy Folbre, and the Center for Popular Economics, *The War on the Poor* (New York: New Press, 1996), p. 20.

86. Ibid.

87. See "Welfare Myths: Fact or Fiction," prepared by the Center on Social Welfare Policy and Law, 1996. E-mail: HN0135@handsnet.org.

88. R. W. Apple, Jr., "His Battle Now Lost, Moynihan Still Cries Out," *New York Times*, August 2, 1996, p. A16.

89. Nina Bernstein, "Giant Companies Entering Race to Run State Welfare Programs," *New York Times*, September 15, 1996, p. A1.

90. Michael Wines and Robert Pear, "President Finds He Has Gained Even if He Lost on Health Care," *New York Times*, July 30, 1996, p. A1.

91. Alison Mitchell, "Despite His Reversals, Clinton Stays Centered," *New York Times*, July 28, 1996, p. A1.

92. For a discussion of the initial Clinton health care proposal, see Theda Skocpol, *Boomerang: Clinton's Health Security Effort and the Turn against Government in U.S. Politics* (New York: W. W. Norton, 1996).

93. Heilemann, "Netizen: Big Brother Bill," 52–53.

94. James Ridgeway, "Green All Over," *Village Voice,* October 8, 1996, p. 26.

95. See Frank Rich, "Let the Trial Begin," *New York Times,* June 1, 1997, p. E17.

96. Reported from a *New York Times* News Poll, June–July 1996, noted in Mitchell, "Clinton Stays Centered," July 28, 1996, p. A1.

97. Steven Holmes, "On Civil Rights, Clinton Steers Bumpy Course between Right and Left," *New York Times,* October 20, 1996, p. A16.

98. For an interesting discussion of the gender bias in news, see Laura Flanders, *Real Majority, Media Minority* (Monroe, Me.: Common Courage Press, 1997).

99. Frank Owen, "Let Them Eat Software," *Village Voice,* February 6, 1996, pp. 31, 32.

100. Alexandra Juhasz, *AIDS TV: Identity, Community, and Alternative Video* (Durham: Duke University Press, 1995). See also Jay Rosen, *Getting the Connections Right: Public Journalism and the Troubles in the Press* (New York: Twentieth Century Fund, 1995).

101. For more information see http://artcon.rutgers.edu/papertiger/nyfma

Notes to Chapter 3

1. Howard Rheingold, *The Virtual Community* (New York: Harper-Perennial, 1993), p. 5.

2. Wayne Ellwood, "Seduced by Technology: The Information Highway," *New Internationalist,* no. 286 (December 1996): 19.

3. Youssef M. Ibrahim, "Rural Finland Becomes the Model of Technology for Everyman," *New York Times,* January 20, 1997, p. D1.

4. Cheryl Coward, "Cyber," *Village Voice,* July 2, 1996, p. 23. See also Jon Katz, "The Digital Citizen," *WIRED* 5.12 (December 1997), for further discussion of who subscribes to the net. According to the sur-

vey used in this article, 87 percent of net users are white, 5 percent are Black, 4 percent are Hispanic (p. 274).

5. Preface to James Brook and Iain A. Boal, eds., *Resisting the Virtual Life* (San Francisco: City Lights, 1995), p. ix.

6. Human Rights Watch Report, "Silencing the Net," *Human Rights Watch,* vol. 8, no. 2 (May 1996): 2, 6.

7. Ellwood, "Seduced by Technology," p. 18.

8. Roger Cohen, "For France, Sagging Self-Image and Esprit," *New York Times,* February 11, 1997, p. A8.

9. Shahidul Alam, "On-line Lifeline," *New Internationalist,* no. 286 (December 1996): 15.

10. Nicholas Baran, "Privatizing Cyberspace," *New Internationalist,* no. 289 (December 1996): 17.

11. Geremie R. Barme and Sang Ye, "The Great Firewall of China," *WIRED* 5.06 (June 1997): 140. For a fuller discussion of the inequalities of access for third-world countries, see Ziauddin Sardar and Jerome R. Ravetz, eds., *Cyberfutures* (New York: New York University Press, 1996).

12. Nicholas Negroponte, *Being Digital* (New York: Vintage, 1995), p. 5.

13. Steve Lohr, "The Great Unplugged Masses Confront the Future," *New York Times,* April 21, 1996, p. E1.

14. Frank Owen, "Let Them Eat Software," *Village Voice,* February 6, 1996, p.31.

15. For a discussion of how living on the net creates virtual communities of real import, see Rheingold, *The Virtual Community.*

16. Todd Oppenheimer, "The Computer Delusion," *Atlantic Monthly,* vol. 280, no. 1 (July 1997): 45–62.

17. David Kine, "The Embedded Internet," *WIRED* 4.10 (October 1996): 98, 102.

18. William Mitchell, *City of Bits* (Cambridge: MIT Press, 1995).

19. Michael Heim, *Electric Language: A Philosophical Study of Word Processing* (New Haven: Yale University Press, 1987), p. 1

20. Timothy Druckrey, ed., *Electronic Culture, Technology and Visual Representation* (New York: Aperture Foundation, 1996).

21. Walter B. Wriston, *The Twilight of Sovereignty* (New York: Scribner's, 1992), pp. 38, 110, xii.

22. N. Katherine Hayles, "Virtual Bodies and Flickering Signifiers," in Druckrey, ed., *Electronic Culture*, p. 261.

23. Michel Foucault, *Power/Knowledge: Selected Interviews and Other Writings*, ed. Colin Gordon (New York: Pantheon, 1972).

24. Karl Marx and Friedrich Engels, *The German Ideology* (New York: International Publishers, 1947)

25. Negroponte, *Being Digital*, p. 230.

26. Theodore Roszak, "Dumbing us Down," *New Internationalist*, no. 286 (December 1996): 13.

27. David Shenk, *Data Smog, Surviving the Information Glut* (San Francisco: Harper Edge, 1997).

28. Dale Spender, *Nattering on the Net: Women, Power and Cyberspace* (North Melbourne, Australia: Spinifex Press, 1995), p. 66.

29. Michael Benedikt, "Cyberspace: Some Proposals," in Benedikt, ed., *Cyberspace: First Steps* (Cambridge: MIT Press, 1991), p. 121.

30. Karen Coyle, "How Hard Can It Be?" in Lynn Cherny and Elizabeth Reba Weise, eds., *Wired Women* (Seattle: Seal Press, 1996), p. 43.

31. Martin Carnoy, introduction to Martin Carnoy, Manuel Castells, Stephen S. Cohen, and Fernando Henrique Cardoso, eds., *The New Global Economy in the Information Age*, (University Park: Pennsylvania State University Press, 1993), p. 2.

32. Ellwood, "Seduced by Technology," p. 18.

33. Jeremy Rivkin, *The End of Work* (New York: G. P. Putnam's Sons, 1995), p. xv.

34. James Petras and Christian Davenport, "The Changing Wealth of the U.S. Ruling Class," *Monthly Review*, vol. 42, no. 7 (December 1990): 33.

35. Paul Wellstone, "If Poverty Is the Question," *The Nation*, April 14, 1997, p. 16.

36. Bill Gates, *The Road Ahead* (New York: Viking, 1995), pp. xii, 41.

37. Bruce Lehman, "The Report of the Working Group on Intellectual Property Rights," in *Intellectual Property and the National Information Infrastructure* (Washington, D.C.: U.S. Patent and Trademark Office, 1995). Also available at http://www.uspto.gov/web/offices/com/doc/ipnii

38. Ibid., pp. 10, 21. See also *Mazer v. Stein*, 347 U.S. 201, 219 (1954).

39. Lehman, "Report," pp. 20, 147. See the related bills S1284 and HR2441. See also Telecommunications Act of 1996, Senate Report no. 104–230 (February 1996).

40. John Perry Barlow, "Stupefyingly Ridiculous," *George*, vol. 1, no. 8 (October 1996): 84.

41. Pamela Samuelson, "Netizen: Confab Clips," *WIRED* 5.03 (March 1997): 62–64. See also John Browning, "Netizen: Copyright Cartel," *WIRED* 5.03 (March 1997): 61–188.

42. Nicholas Baran, *Inside the Information Superhighway Revolution* (Scottsdale, Az.: Coriolis Group Books, 1995), p. 38.

43. Steven E. Miller, *Civilizing Cyberspace* (New York: Addison Wesley, 1996), pp. 106–9.

44. Ibid., p. 110.

45. Ibid., pp. 141, 143.

46. Neal Gabler, "Bill Gates Goes Vertical," *New York Times*, June 12, 1997, p. A23.

47. Robert W. McChesney, "Digital Highway Robbery," *The Nation*, April 21, 1997, p. 22. See also Bob Dole, "Giving Away the Airwaves," *New York Times*, March 27, 1997, p. A29.

48. Claudia Dreifus, "The Cyber-Maxims of Esther Dyson," *New York Times Magazine*, July 7, 1996, p. 19.

49. A statement by Elizabeth Lewis cited in Carl Malamud, "Building a Park on RSA," *WIRED* 4.10 (October 1996): 133.

50. Kali Tal, "Life Behind the Screen," *WIRED* 4.10 (October 1996): 134.

51. Louise K. Wilson, "Cyberwar, God and Televison: Interview with Paul Virilio," in Druckrey, ed., *Electronic Culture*, p. 322.

52. Mark Dery, *Escape Velocity: Cyberculture at the End of the Century* (New York: Grove Press, 1996), p. 6.

53. Allucquere Rosanne Stone, *The War of Desire and Technology at the Close of the Mechanical Age* (Cambridge: MIT Press, 1996), p. 12.

54. Mark Dery, "The Cult of the Mind," *New York Times Magazine*, September 28, 1997, p. 94.

55. Kim H. Veltman, "Electronic Media: The Rebirth of Perspective and the Fragmentation of Illusion," in Druckrey, ed., *Electronic Culture*, p. 223.

56. Vilem Flusser, "Digital Apparition," in Druckrey, ed., *Electronic Culture*, pp. 242–244.

57. Benedikt, "Cyberspace: Some Proposals," p. 122.

58. Interview with Donna Haraway, by Hari Kunzru, "You Are Borg," *WIRED* 5.02 (February 1997): 155–59. See also Haraway, "Manifesto for Cyborgs," *Socialist Review*, no. 80 (1985): 65–108, reprinted in Linda Nicholson, ed., *Feminism/Postmodernism* (New York: Routledge, 1990), pp. 190–233.

59. Dery, *Escape Velocity*, p. 241. See also Naomi Wolf, *The Beauty Myth* (New York: Random House, 1991).

60. See Mark Dery's interesting discussion/critique of Naomi Wolf in *Escape Velocity*, pp. 240–42.

61. Kunzru, "You Are Borg," p. 157.

62. Anne Balsamo, "Feminism for the Incurably Informed," in Mark Dery, ed., *Flame Wars: The Discourse of Cyberculture* (Durham: Duke University Press, 1994), p. 147.

63. Marcos Novak, "Liquid Architectures in Cyberspace," in Benedikt, ed., *Cyberspace*, p. 226.

64. Lynn Hershman Leeson, "R.U.Sirius Interview," in Leeson, ed., *Clicking In: Hot Links to a Digital Culture* (Seattle: Bay Press, 1996), p. 56.

65. Lynn Hershman Leeson, "Jaron Lanier Interview," in Leeson, ed., *Clicking In*, p. 45. See also Steven G. Jones, ed., *Cybersociety* (Thousand Oaks, Calif.: Sage Pub., 1995).

66. Susie Bright, *Susie Bright's Sexual Reality: A Virtual Sex World*

Reader (San Francisco: Cleis Press, 1992), pp. 67, 68. See also her *Sexwise* (San Francisco: Cleis Press, 1995).

67. I thank Miriam Brody for this insight.

68. David Tomas, "Old Rituals for New Space: Rites de Passage and William Gibson's Cultural Model of Cyberspace,", in Benedikt, ed., *Cyberspace*, p. 32. See also William Gibson, *Neuromancer* (New York: Ace Books, 1984), and his *Count Zero*, (New York: Ace Books, 1987).

69. Vivian Sobchack, "New Age Mutant Ninja Hackers: Reading Mondo 2000," in Dery, ed., *Flame Wars*, p. 20.

70. Michael Heim, "The Erotic Ontology of Cyberspace," in Benedikt, ed., *Cyberspace*, p. 74.

71. Ellen Ullman, "Come in, CQ: The Body on the Wire," in Lynn Cherny and Elizabeth Reba Weise, eds., *Wired Women* (Seattle: Seal Press, 1996), p. 12.

72. Meghan Daum, "Virtual Love," *New Yorker,* August 25–September 1, 1997, pp. 81, 82.

73. Katie Hafner, "The Epic Saga of the Well," *WIRED* 5.05 (May 1997): 109.

74. Elizabeth Reba Weise, "A Thousand Aunts with Modems," in Cherny and Weise, eds., *Wired Women*, p. xii.

75. Richard E. Sclove, *Democracy and Technology* (New York: Guilford Press, 1995), p. 80.

76. McKenzie Wark, *Virtual Geography* (Bloomington: Indiana University Press, 1994), p. vii.

77. Arjun Appadurai, *Modernity at Large* (Minneapolis: University of Minnesota Press, 1997), p. 22.

78. Sheldon Renan, "The Net and the Future of Being Fictive," in Leeson, ed., *Clicking In*, p. 67.

79. Lynn Hershman Leeson, "Interview with Joichi and Mizuko Ito," in Leeson, ed., *Clicking In*, p. 79.

80. Simon Davies, "Hacked Off," *WIRED* 2.07 (July 1996): 14.

81. Gates, *The Road Ahead*, p. 258.

82. Chris Hedges, "Serbs' Answer to Tyranny? Get on the Web," *New York Times,* December 8, 1996, p. A1.

83. Sherry Turkle, *Life on the Screen* (New York: Simon and Schuster, 1995), especially chap. 6. See also Jonathan Wallace and Mark Mangan, *Sex, Laws, and Cyber-space* (New York: Henry Holt, 1996), for a careful discussion of censorship on the net.

84. Dery, *Escape Velocity*, p. 201.

85. Shannon McRae, "Sex, Text and the Virtual Body," in Cherny and Weise, eds., *Wired Women*, p. 245.

86. Dery, *Escape Velocity*, pp. 210–12, 219.

87. Leeson, "R. U. Sirius Interview," in Leeson, ed., *Clicking In*, p. 60.

88. Claudia Springer, *Electronic Eros: Bodies and Desire in the Postindustrial Age* (Austin: University of Texas Press, 1996), pp. 19, 8, 9.

89. Sobchack, "New Age Mutant Ninja Hackers," p. 20.

90. Lori Kendall, "MUDder? I Hardly Know 'Er! Adventures of a Feminist MUDder," in Cherny and Weise, eds., *Wired Women*, p. 218.

91. R. U. Sirius and St. Jude, *How to Mutate and Take Over the World* (New York: Ballantine, 1996), pp. 64–77.

92. Robert Maxwell Young, "Laboratories of the Self," *WIRED* 2.07 (July 1996): 27.

93. Debra Michals, "Cyber-Rape: How Virtual Is It?" *Ms. Magazine*, vol. 7, no. 5 (March–April 1997): 69.

94. Paulina Borsook, "The Memoirs of a Token: An Aging Berkeley Feminist Examines *WIRED*," in Cherny and Weise, eds., *Wired Women*, p. 29.

95. Michele Evard, "'So Please Stop, Thank You': Girls Online," in Cherny and Weise, eds., *Wired Women*, p. 188.

96. Coyle, "How Hard Can It Be?" p. 47.

97. Stephanie Brail, "The Price of Admission: Harassment and Free Speech in the Wild, Wild West," in Cherny and Weise, eds., *Wired Women*, p. 148.

98. Laurel A. Sutton, "Cocktails and Thumbtacks in the Old West: What Would Emily Post Say?" in Cherny and Weise, eds., *Wired Women*, p. 171.

99. Quoted in Carla Sinclair, *Netchick* (New York: Henry Holt, 1996), pp. 87, 95.

100. Donna Riley, "Sex, Fear and Condescension on Campus: Cybercensorship at Carnegie Mellon," in Cherny and Weise, eds., *Wired Women*, p. 163.

101. G. Beato, "Girl Games," *WIRED* 5.04 (April 1997): 100.

102. Neil MacFarquhar, "With Mixed Feelings, Iran Tiptoes to the Internet," *New York Times*, October 8, 1996, p. A4.

102. St. Jude in R. U. Sirius and St. Jude, *How to Mutate and Takeover the World*, p. 39.

103. Human Rights Watch Report, "Silencing the Net," 10–18.

105. Miller, *Civilizing Cyberspace*, p. 183.

106. See the *Libraries for the Future Overview*, April 21, 1997, available from Librarians for the Future, 121 West 27th St., Suite 1102, New York, N.Y. 10001.

107. Balsamo, "Feminism for the Incurably Informed," p. 138.

108. Stone, *Desire and Technology*, p. 36. See also Marshall McLuhan and Quentin Fiore, *War and Peace in the Global Village* (1968; reprint, San Francisco: Hardwired, 1997), for one of the earliest discussions of computers as extensions of the body.

109. Peter Lewis, "Second Ruling Opposes Rules on Indecency on the Internet," *New York Times*, July 30, 1996, p. A7.

110. "Excerpts from Opinions against Law on Internet," *New York Times*, June 12, 1996, p. B11. See also *American Civil Liberties Union v. Janet Reno*, 929 F. Supp. 824 (E. D. Pa. 1996).

111. Linda Greenhouse, "Decency Act Fails," *New York Times*, June 27, 1997, p. A1. See: 65LW4715–4730.

112. Newt Gingrich, *To Renew America* (New York: Harper Collins, 1995).

113. Andrew L. Shapiro, "Privacy for Sale: Peddling Data on the Internet," *The Nation*, June 23, 1997, p. 12.

114. Nicholas Baran, "Privatization of Telecommunications," *Monthly Review*, vol. 48, no. 3 (July–August 1996); 61, 68.

115. Miller, *Civilizing Cyberspace*, p. 176.

116. Jessie Scanlon, "Hacking the Clinton White House," *WIRED* 4.11 (November 1996): 69.

117. Miller, *Civilizing Cyberspace*, p. 119.

118. Arthur Kroker and Marilouise Kroker, "Code Warriors: Bunkering In and Dumbing Down," in Leeson, ed., *Clicking In*, pp. 251–255.

119. For reports of the MacBride Roundtable, contact http://people.rfem.or.kr/macbride/ See also William Harley, *Creative Compromise: The MacBride Commission* (New York: University Press of America, 1993).

120. Guillermo Gómez-Peña, "The Virtual Barrio @ the Other Frontier (or the Chicano Interneta," in Leeson, ed., *Clicking In*, p. 179.

121. The charter can be found at hamelink@antenna.n1@IN@ IC2 Another location for information on PCC is http://www.waag.org/pcc.

122. Miller, *Civilizing Cyberspace*, p. 372.

123. Many of these concerns have been voiced by Ursula Franklin in her discussion of democratic decision-making and new technologies, as presented in Ellwood, "Seduced by Technology," p. 10. See also Ursula Franklin, *The Real World of Technology* (Toronto: Anansi Press, 1990).

Notes to Chapter 4

1. Paul Virilio, *Open Sky* (London: Verso, 1997), p. 21.

2. Cynthia Enloe, "Silicon Tricks and the Two Dollar Woman," *New Internationalist*, no. 227 (January 1992): 12.

3. Introduction to Rob Wilson and Wimal Dissanayake, eds., *Global/Local: Cultural Production and the Transnational Imaginary* (Durham: Duke University Press, 1996), pp. 2, 5.

4. Virilio, *Open Sky*, pp. 69, 135.

5. Arjun Appadurai, *Modernity at Large: Cultural Dimensions of Globalization* (Minneapolis: University of Minnesota Press, 1997), p. 82.

6. Introduction to Wilson and Dissanayake, eds., *Global/Local*, p. 3.

7. Ellen Meiksins Wood, "Modernity, Postmodernity, or Capitalism?" *Monthly Review,* vol. 48, no. 3 (July–August 1996): 38.

8. Appadurai makes a similar argument in *Modernity at Large*.

9. For a full accounting of this argument, see Zillah Eisenstein, *HA-TREDS: Racialized and Sexualized Conflicts in the 21st Century* (New York: Routledge, 1996), especially chap. 3.

10. Quoted in Ellen Meiksins Wood, "Issues of Class and Culture: An Interview with Aijaz Ahmad," *Monthly Review,* vol. 48, no. 5 (October 1996): 19.

11. Steven Holmes, "Income Disparity Between Poorest and Richest Rises," *New York Times,* July 20, 1996, p. A1.

12. Rosi Braidotti, Ewa Charkiewicz, Sabine Hausler, and Saskia Wieringa, *Women, the Environment and Sustainable Development* (London: Zed Books, 1994), p. 1.

13. Benjamin Barber, *Jihad vs. McWorld* (New York: Random House, 1995), p. 88.

14. Jeremy Rifkin, *The End of Work* (New York: G. P. Putnam's Sons, 1995), p. 149.

15. Anthony Giddens, *The Consequences of Modernity* (Stanford: Stanford University Press, 1990), p. 19.

16. Kenichi Ohmae, *The Borderless World* (New York: Harper Business, 1990).

17. Armand Mattelart, *Mapping World Communication* (Minneapolis: University of Minnesota Press, 1994), pp. 13, 14, 15.

18. Jerry Gray, "Senate G.O.P. Unveils Tax Plan, A $245 Billion Cut," *New York Times,* October 14, 1995, p. A1. See also James Rinehart, "The Ideology of Competitiveness," *Monthly Review,* vol. 47, no. 5 (October 1995): 14–23.

19. See Zillah Eisenstein, *The Female Body and the Law* (Berkeley: University of California Press, 1989), and *The Color of Gender* (Berkeley: University of California Press, 1994).

20. See Major Garrett, "Beyond the Contract," *Mother Jones,* vol. 20, no. 2 (March–April, 1995): 52–58; Bob Herbert, "Asleep at the

Revolution," *New York Times*, November 6, 1995, p. A17; and Robert Pear, "Shifting Where the Buck Stops," *New York Times*, October 29, 1995, p. D1.

21. See Bob Herbert, "Don't Call It Welfare Reform," *New York Times*, September 25, 1995, p. A15; Daniel Patrick Moynihan, "Congress Builds a Coffin," *New York Review of Books*, January 11, 1996, pp. 33–36; and Robin Toner, "Senate Approves Welfare Plan That Would End Aid Guarantee," *New York Times*, September 20, 1995, p. A1.

22. Bob Herbert, "Kiss and Cut," *New York Times*, October 23, 1995, p. A15.

23. Melvin Konner, "A Giant Leap Backward," *New York Times*, October 13, 1995, p. A23.

24. John Kennedy, Jr., "Editorial," *George*, vol. 1, no. 1 (October–November 1995): 10.

25. David Korten, "The Limits of the Earth," *The Nation*, Special Issue: *It's the Global Economy, Stupid*, July 15–22, 1996, p. 16.

26. For a discussion of the relative autonomy of the patriarchal state see: Zillah Eisenstein, *Feminism and Sexual Equality: Crisis in Liberal America* (New York: Monthly Review Press, 1984), especially chap. 4.

27. For discussions of statist aspects of patriarchy, see ibid; Zillah Eisenstein, *The Radical Future of Liberal Feminism* (Boston: Northeastern University Press, 1981, 1993); and Eisenstein, *HATREDS*. See also Rosalind Pollack Petchesky, *Abortion and Woman's Choice: The State, Sexuality, and Reproductive Freedom*, rev. ed. (Boston: Northeastern University Press, 1990).

28. Michael Janofsky, "At Million Woman March, Focus Is on Family," *New York Times*, October 26, 1997), p. A1.

29. Francis Fukuyama, *Trust: The Social Virtues and the Creation of Prosperity* (New York: Free Press, 1995), pp. 336, 337.

30. Aijaz Ahmad, "The Politics of Literary Postcoloniality," *Race and Class*, vol. 36, no. 3 (January–March 1995): 11, 12.

31. Martin Carnoy, "Multinationals in a Changing World Economy: Whither the Nation-Sate?" in Martin Carnoy, Manuel Castells,

Stephen S. Cohen, and Fernando Henrique Cardoso, eds., *The New Global Economy in the Information Age* (University Park: Pennsylvania State University Press, 1996), p. 88.

32. Fukuyama, *Trust*, p. 344.

33. Geraldine Heng, "'A Great Way to Fly': Nationalism, the State, and the Varieties of Third-World Feminism," in M. Jacqui Alexander and Chandra Talpade Mohanty, eds., *Feminist Genealogies, Colonial Legacies, Democratic Futures* (New York: Routledge, 1997), p. 33.

34. Wood, "Issues of Class and Conflict," pp. 16, 17.

35. William Greider, *One World, Ready or Not* (New York: Simon and Schuster, 1997), p. 187. See also Paul Krugman, *Peddling Prosperity* (New York: W. W. Norton, 1994).

36. Edmund L. Andrews, "68 Nations Agree to Widen Markets in Communications," *New York Times*, February 16, 1997, p. A1.

37. Nicholas Negroponte, *Being Digital* (New York: Vintage, 1995), pp. 238, 240.

38. John Browning, "Netizen: I Encrypt, Therefore I Am," *WIRED* 5.11 (November 1997): 65.

39. The "Subcommittee on Terrorism, Technology, and Government Information" report prepared for the Judiciary of the U.S. Senate examines the problem of the availability of bomb-making information on the internet. See report no. J-104–25, May 11, 1995, (Washington: U.S. Government Printing Office, 1996). See also the report "Internet Crimes Affecting Consumers," no. J-105–5, March 19, 1997, prepared for the same committee.

40. Peter Golding, "World Wide Wedge: Division and Contradiction in the Global Information Infrastructure," *Monthly Review*, vol. 48, no. 3 (July–August 1996): 82.

41. William K. Tabb, "Globalization Is An Issue, The Power of Capital Is the Issue," *Monthly Review*, vol. 49, no. 2 (June 1997): 27.

42. Rifkin, *The End of Work*, p. 182.

43. Holly Sklar, *Chaos or Community?* (Boston: South End Press, 1995), p. 37.

44. According to Robert Brenner of U.C.L.A., cited in Alexander

Cockburn, "The Witch Hunt and the Crash," *The Nation*, November 17, 1997, p. 9.

45. Jeremy Rifkin, "Civil Society in the Information Age," *The Nation*, February 26, 1996, p. 11.

46. Cockburn, "The Witch Hunt and the Crash," p. 9.

47. Rifkin, *The End of Work*, pp. xvi, 3, 134, 144.

48. Ibid., pp. 71, 88, 89, 126, 127, 167, 16.

49. Saskia Sassen, "Whose City Is It? Globalization and the Formation of New Claims," *Public Culture*, Special Issue: *Cities and Citizenship*, vol. 8, no. 2 (winter 1996): 208. See also Reebee Garofalo, "Whose World, What Beat?" *Radical America*, vol. 25, no. 4 (October–December, 1991): 25–40.

50. Saskia Sassen, *The Global City* (Princeton: Princeton University Press, 1991), pp. 20–23.

51. Eward Soja, *Postmodern Geographies* (London: Verso, 1989), p. 217.

52. Richard Appelbaum, "Multiculturalism and Flexibility: Some New Directions in Global Capitalism," in Avery Gordon and Christopher Newfield, eds., *Mapping Multiculturalism* (Minneapolis: University of Minnesota Press, 1996), p. 298.

53. Saskia Sassen, *Cities in a World Economy* (Thousand Oaks, Calif.: Pine Forge Press, 1994), p. 53.

54. Richard Appelbaum, "Multiculturalism and Flexibility," in Gordon and Newfield, eds., *Mapping Multiculturalism*, p. 309.

55. Marc Cooper, "The Heartland's Raw Deal," *The Nation*, February 3, 1997, pp. 11–18.

56. Deborah Sontag, "For Poorest, Life 'Trapped in a Cage,'" *New York Times*, October 6, 1996, p. A1.

57. Rick Bragg, "Defying Odds in Mississippi, Black Carries G.O.P. Torch," *New York Times*, June 24, 1996, p. A1.

58. Manuel Castells, "The Informational Economy and the New International Division of Labor," in Carnoy et al., eds., *The New Global Economy in the Information Age*, p. 27.

59. Fernando Henrique Cardoso, "North-South Relations in the

Present Context: A New Dependency?" in Carnoy et al., eds., *The New Global Economy in the Information Age*, p. 156.

60. Holly Sklar and Chuck Collins, "Forbes 400 World Series," *The Nation*, October 12, 1997,. p. 6.

61. Rifkin, *The End of Work*, p. 177.

62. Simon Head, "The New Ruthless Economy," *New York Review of Books*, February 29, 1996, p. 51.

63. Tom Petruno, "A Return to Rational Rates," *Los Angeles Times*, January 29, 1992, p. D1. See also "Compensation and the I.R.S.: It's Not the 'Good' Old Days," *New York Times*, April 14, 1996, p. F8; and Kevin Phillips, *Boiling Point* (New York: Random House, 1993).

64. Louis Uchitelle, "1995 Was Good for Companies, and Better for a Lot of C.E.O.'s," *New York Times*, March 29, 1996, p. A1.

65. Head, "The New Ruthless Economy," p. 47.

66. David Bacon, "For a Labor Economy," *The Nation*, April 1, 1996, p. 14.

67. Information packet on the Gap, from the National Labor Committee, Education Fund in Support of Worker and Human Rights in Central America, 15 Union Square, New York, N.Y. 10003.

68. Steven Greenhouse, "Nike Shoe Plant in Vietnam Is Called Unsafe for Workers," *New York Times*, November 8, 1997, p. A1.

69. Bob Herbert, "Nike's Pyramid Scheme," *New York Times,* June 10, 1996, p. A17.

70. Bob Herbert, "Trampled Dreams," *New York Times,* July 12, 1996, p. A27.

71. Bob Herbert, "From Sweatshops to Aerobics," *New York Times,* June 24, 1996, p. A15.

72. William Greider, "One World, Ready or Not," *Rolling Stone,* February 6, 1997, p. 40. See also his book of the same title.

73. Eyal Press, "Barbie's Betrayal," *The Nation*, December 30, 1996, pp. 11–16.

74. See "Disney: Urgent Action Alert," May 6, 1997. Available from the National Labor Committee, 275 7th Ave, New York, N.Y. 10001.

75. "Mickey Mouse Linked to Support of Worker and Human

Rights in Central America," October 10, 1996, news release, available from the National Labor Coalition.

76. William Falk, "Dirty Little Secrets," *Newsday*, June 16, 1996, pp. A4, A5.

75. Steven Greenhouse, "Voluntary Rules on Apparel Labor Proving Elusive," *New York Times*, February 1, 1997, p. A1.

78. Clifford Cobb, Ted Halstead, and Jonathan Rowe, "If the GDP Is Up, Why Is American Down?" *Atlantic Monthly*, vol. 276, no. 4 (October 1995): 65–67.

79. Amy Spindler, "It's a Face-Lifted, Tummy-Tucked Jungle out There," *New York Times*, June 9, 1996, p. F1.

80. Barbara Koeppel, "Newfangled Cobra," *The Nation*, June 24, 1996, p. 5.

81. Korten, "The Limits of the Earth," p. 18.

82. David M. Gordon, *Fat and Mean* (New York: Free Press, 1996), pp. 146, 153.

83. See Ralph Estes, *Tyranny of the Bottom Line: Why Corporations Make Good People Do Bad Things* (San Francisco: Berrett-Koehler, 1996); and Paul Krugman, *Pop Internationalism* (Cambridge: MIT Press, 1996).

84. Rick Bragg, "Buses Again Trouble Civil Rights Veterans," *New York Times*, June 16, 1996, p. A12.

85. Louis Uchitelle and N. R. Kleinfeld, "On the Battlefields of Business, Millions of Casualties," *New York Times*, March 3, 1996, p. A1.

86. John Tagliabue, "In Europe, A Wave of Layoffs Stuns White-Collar Workers," *New York Times*, June 20, 1996, p. A1.

87. Jason DeParle, "Class is No Longer a Four-Letter Word," *New York Times Magazine*, March 17, 1996, pp. 40–43.

88. Michael Winerip, "A Union Standing Fast Now Stands to Lose," *New York Times*, June 12, 1996, p. A16.

89. Uchitelle and Kleinfeld, "On the Battlefields of Business," p. A1.

90. Jim Robbins, "U.S. Budget Cuts Imperil Remote Town's Lifeline," *New York Times*, June 16, 1996, p. A14.

91. Sara Rimer, "Hometown Feels Less Like Home," *New York Times,* March 6, 1996, p. A1.

92. Uchitelle and N. R. Kleinfeld, "On the Battlefields of Business" p. 29.

93. N. R. Keinfield, "The Company as Family, No More," *New York Times,* March 4, 1996, p. A12.

94. Appadurai, *Modernity at Large,* p. 22.

95. Partha Chatterjee, "Beyond the Nation? Or Within?" *Economic and Political Weekly,* January 4–11, 1997, p. 30. See Chatterjee's interesting critique of Appadurai's notion of 'beyond' the nation.

96. Ben Anderson developed the notion of dual identity in his talk, "E-Mail Nationalism," at Cornell University, January 31, 1997.

97. Barbara Crossette, "Democracies Love Peace, Don't They?" *New York Times,* June 1, 1997, p. E3.

98. Daniel Singer, "The Cliffhanger in France," *The Nation,* June 16, 1997, pp. 15–20.

99. Hochul Sonn, "The 'Late Blooming' of the South Korean Labor Movement," *Monthly Review,* vol. 49, no. 3 (July–August 1997): 117.

100. Robert Reich, "The Politics of Layoff: In Search of a Message," *New York Times,* March 8, 1996, p. A1.

101. Robert Reich, *Locked in the Cabinet* (New York: Alfred A. Knopf, 1997).

102. Michael Tanzer, "Globalizing the Economy: The Influence of the International Monetary Fund and the World Bank," *Monthly Review,* vol. 47, no. 4 (September 1995): 1.

103. Quoted in Steven Greenhouse, "New Fire for Labor," *New York Times,* October 26, 1995, p. A1.

104. Ian Fisher, "Workers March to Protest Medicare and Medicaid Cutbacks," *New York Times,* November 3, 1995, p. B3.

105. Bob Herbert, "Strength in Numbers," *New York Times,* November 3, 1995, p. A29.

106. Joy Gordon, "Cuba's Entrepreneurial Socialism," *Atlantic Monthly,* vol. 279, no. 1 (January 1997): 18–30.

107. Andreas Jorgensen, "Efficiency and Welfare under Capitalism: Denmark vs. The U.S., A Short Comparison," *Monthly Review,* vol. 48, no. 7 (February 1997): 36–40.

108. Grace Lee Boggs, "Martin and Malcolm: How Shall We Honor Our Heroes?" *Monthly Review,* vol. 49, no. 2 (June 1997): 15.

109. Pierre Pradervand, *Listening to Africa* (New York: Praeger, 1989), pp. 168, 199, 200.

110. Ibid., p. 17.

Notes to Chapter 5

1. Paul Ekins, *A New World Order: Grassroots Movements for Global Change* (New York: Routledge, 1992), p. 74.

2. Vanessa Baird, "We've Only Just Begun," *New Internationalist,* no. 227 (January 1992): 5.

3. The Fourth World Conference on Women, Beijing, China, September 4–15, 1995, sponsored by the United Nations.

4. Carolyn Merchant, *Earthcare* (New York: Routledge, 1995), pp. 146, 166.

5. From the Report *Women and Economic Decision-Making,* Division for the Advancement of Women/Secretariat for the Fourth World Conference on Women, November 11, 1994. Available from the United Nations, Two United Nations Plaza, New York, N.Y. 10017.

6. Akbar S. Ahmed, *Postmodernism and Islam* (New York: Routledge, 1992), p. 99.

7. Report of the Secretary-General, *From Nairobi to Beijing* (New York: United Nations, 1995), pp. 254, 257.

8. Ibid., p. 259.

9. Jill Petty, "Only 5 of 190 World Leaders Are Women. How are they Doing?" *Ms. Magazine,* vol. 6, no. 5 (March–April 1996), pp. 20, 22. See also *From Nairobi to Beijing,* pp. 45–80; and Margaret A. Schuler, ed., *From Basic Needs to Basic Rights* (Washington, D.C.: Institute for Women, Law and Development, 1995).

10. See Peter Adamson, "A Failure of Imagination," p. 3, and

Vulimiri Ramalingaswami, Urban Jonsson, and Jon Rohde, "The Asian Enigma: Nutrition Commentary," p. 15, both in *The Progress of Nations*, 1996 (New York: UNICEF House, 1996); Jeanne Vickers, *Women and the World Economic Crisis* (London: Zed Books, 1991), p. 27; and Barbara Crossette, "New Tally of World Tragedy: Women Who Die Giving Life," *New York Times*, June 11, 1996, p. A1.

11. Nicholas D. Kristof, "Asian Childhoods Sacrificed to Prosperity's Lust," *New York Times*, April 14, 1996, p. A1.

12. Data compiled from United Nations sources by Women's Feature Service, reported in "Vital Signs," *The Nation*, September 11, 1995, p. 234.

13. Ramalingaswami, Jonsson, and Rohde, *The Progress of Nations*, 1996, p. 11.

14. Robert Friedman, "India's Shame," *The Nation*, April 8, 1996, pp. 11–20.

15. *From Nairobi to Beijing*, p. 66.

16. Julie Mertus and Jasmina Tesanovic, introduction to Julie Mertus, Jasmina Tesanovic, Habiba Metikos, and Rada Boric, eds., *The Suitcase: Refugee Voices from Bosnia and Croatia* (Berkeley: University of California Press, 1997), p. 8.

17. From the "Poverty Factsheet," *Committee for the '95 World Conference on Women*, September 4–15, Beijing, China. Available from the United Nations.

18. *The World's Women, 1995, Trends and Statistics* (New York: United Nations, 1995), p. xviii.

19. Statement by Mrs. Gertrude Mongella, assistant secretary-general of the Fourth World Conference on Women, delivered to the World Summit on Social Development, Copenhagen, Denmark, March 6–12, 1995, p. 3. Available from the United Nations.

20. *The World's Women*, 1995, p. 48.

21. Claudia von Werlhof, "The Proletarian is Dead: Long Live the Housewife!" in Maria Mies, Veronika Bennholdt-Thomsen and Claudia von Werlhof, eds., *Women: The Last Colony* (London: Zed Books, 1988), p. 181.

22. Maria Mies, introduction to Mies, Bennholdt-Thomsen, and von Werlhof, eds., *Women: The Last Colony,* pp. 1, 26.

23. *The Advancement of Women: Notes for Speakers,* a pamphlet issued by the Department of Public Information, United Nations, pp. 14–27. Prepared for the Fourth World Congress on Women, Beijing, 1995.

24. Sheila Rowbotham and Swasti Mitter, eds., *Dignity and Daily Bread* (New York: Routledge, 1994).

25. Amy Waldman, "Labor's New Face," *Nation,* September 22, 1997, p. 16.

26. Dave Broad, "Globalization versus Labor," *Monthly Review,* vol. 47, no. 7 (December 1995): 26, 27. See also Maria Mies, *Patriarchy and Accumulation on a World Scale* (London: Zed Books, 1986); and Joni Seager, *The State of Women in the World Atlas* (New York: Penguin, 1997).

27. *Crossroads,* Special Issue: "Women's Activism after Beijing," no. 59 (March 1996).

28. *The Advancement of Women,* pp. 6, 23.

29. Leslie Sklair, *Sociology of the Global System* (Baltimore: Johns Hopkins University Press, 1991), p. 109.

30. Maria Mies, "Capitalist Development and Subsistence Production: Rural Women in India," in Mies, Bennholdt-Thomsen, and von Werlhof, eds., *Women: The Last Colony,* p. 45.

31. Introduction to Elisabeth Prugl and Eileen Boris, eds., *Homeworkers in Global Perspective* (New York: Routledge, 1996), pp. 4, 5.

32. Elisabeth Prugl, "Home-Based Producers in Development Discourse," in Prugl and Boris, eds., *Homeworkers in Global Perspective,* pp. 46, 47.

33. Jeanne Hahn, "Feminization through Flexible Labor," in Prugl and Boris, eds., *Homeworkers in Global Perspective,* p. 223.

34. Christina Gringeri, "Making Cadillacs and Buicks for General Motors," in Prugl and Boris, eds., *Homeworkers in Global Perspective,* pp. 180–184, 187.

35. Broad, "Globalization versus Labor," p. 26.

36. Veronika Bennholdt-Thomsen, "Why Do Housewives Continue to Be Created in the Third World Too?" in Mies, Bennholdt-Thomsen, and von Werlhof, eds., *Women: The Last Colony,* pp. 159, 166.

37. Veronika Bennholdt-Thomsen, "The Future of Women's Work and Violence against Women", in Mies, Bennholdt-Thomsen, and von Werlhof, eds., *Women: The Last Colony,* p. 127.

38. "Vital Signs," *The Nation,* September 11, 1995, p. 234.

39. Sklair, *Sociology of the Global System,* pp. 99, 109.

40. Marisol Ruiz, "Free Slave Zones," *Crossroads,* Special Issue: Women's Activism after Beijing, no. 59 (March 1996): 11.

41. Miriam Ching Louie, "Breaking the Cycle," *Crossroads,* Special Issue: Women's Activism after Beijing, no. 59 (March 1996): 22.

42. Bob Herbert, "In Deep Denial," *New York Times,* October 13, 1995, p. A21.

43. Statement from a photography exhibit by Cindy Andrew, *Rights and Realities,* Canadian Museum of Contemporary Photography, September 14– December 10, 1995.

44. Quoted in the documentary film *Zoned for Slavery,* dir. by David Belle, Katherine Kean, and Rudi Stern. Available from the National Labor Committee, 15 Union Square, New York, N.Y. 10003. See also "Mexico: No Guarantees, Sex Discrimination in Mexico's Maquilladora Sector," *Human Rights Watch/Women's Rights Project,* vol. 8, no. 6 (August 1996).

45. Data is sited in a UNITE (Union of Needletrades, Industrial, and Textile Employees) newsletter, February 1997.

46. Cynthia Enloe, "Silicon Tricks and the Two Dollar Woman," *New Internationalist,* no. 227 (January 1992): 12.

47. Geraldine Heng, "'A Great Way to Fly'": Nationalism, the State, and the Varieties of Third-World Feminism," in M. Jacqui Alexander and Chandra Talpade Mohanty, eds., *Feminist Genealogies, Colonial Legacies, Democratic Futures* (New York: Routledge, 1997), p. 32.

48. Schuler, *From Basic Needs to Basic Rights,* pp. 64, 159, 162.

49. *The World's Women, 1995,* p. 5.

50. *Women's Agenda for Action* (Washington, D.C.: ALT-WID, Alternative Women in Development, 1996), p. 6. Available from Alternative Women in Development, 3700 13th St. NE, Washington, D.C. 20017.

51. Steven Stark, "Gap Politics," *Atlantic Monthly*, vol. 278, no. 1 (July 1996): 71–80.

52. The Contract is sponsored by the Women's Environment and Development Organization (WEDO) and is available from WEDO, 845 Third Avenue, 15th floor, New York, N.Y., 10022.

53. For a fuller discussion of neoconservative privatization of the state, see Zillah Eisenstein, *The Female Body and the Law* (Berkeley: University of California Press, 1988), and *The Color of Gender* (Berkeley: University of California Press, 1994).

54. Gayle Kirshenbaum, "Why All But One Woman Senator Voted against Welfare," *Ms. Magazine*, vol. 6, no. 5 (March–April 1996):.16.

55. Kristin Luker, *Dubious Conceptions: The Politics of Teenage Pregnancy* (Cambridge: Harvard University Press, 1996), p. 8.

56. As quoted in Nina Burleigh, "Secret Agents," *George*, vol. 1 (February–March 1996): 88.

57. See Susan Faludi's interesting discussion, "Swedish Sojourn," *Ms. Magazine*, vol. 6, no. 6 (March–April 1996): 67–71.

58. B. Drummond Ayres, "Women in Washington Statehouse," *New York Times*, April 14, 1997, p. A1.

59. Esther Adagala and Wambui Kiai, "Folk, Interpersonal and Mass Media: The Experience of Women in Africa," in Margaret Gallagher and Lilia Quindoza-Santiago, eds., *Women Empowering Communication* (Thailand: Open University Press, n.d.), pp. 11–36.

60. See Zillah Eisenstein, *HATREDS: Sexualized and Racialized Conflicts in the 21st Century* (New York: Routledge, 1996).

61. Mervat F. Hatem, "Privatization and the Demise of State Feminism in Egypt," in Pamela Sparr, ed., *Mortgaging Women's Lives: Feminist Critiques of Structural Adjustment* (London: Zed Books, 1994), pp. 47, 48.

62. Grace Lee Boggs, "Martin and Malcolm: How Shall We Honor Our Heroes?" *Monthly Review*, vol. 49, no. 2 (June 1997): 15.

63. Reed Boland, *Promoting Reproductive Rights: A Global Mandate* (New York: The Center for Reproductive Law and Policy, 1997).

64. Barbara Crossette, "Women Say China Stalls on Parley," *New York Times*, July 30, 1995, p. A4, and her "The Second Sex in the Third World," *New York Times*, September 10, 1995, p. E1; Seth Faison, "Meeting of Women Says Surveillance by China Must End", *New York Times*, September 2, 1995, p. A1, and his "Women of the World Disperse to What?" *New York Times*, September 17, 1995, p. E3; Geraldine Ferraro, "Women's Rights, Human Rights," *New York Times*, August 22, 1995, p. A15; Robin Morgan, "Dispatch from Beijing," *Ms. Magazine*, vol. 6, no. 4, (January–February 1996): 12–21; Camille Paglia, "A White Liberal Women's Conference," *New York Times*, September 1, 1995, p. A15; Todd Purdum, "The Clintons Back Parley on Women," *New York Times*, August 27, 1995, p. A10; Patrick Tyler, "At U.N. Women's Meeting, an Outbreak of Harmony," *New York Times*, September 9, 1995, p. A2, and his "Beijing Women's Forum Agrees on 'Platform for Action,'" *New York Times*, September 15, 1995, p. A3.

65. "A Brief Analysis of the UN Fourth World Conference on Women, Beijing Declaration, and Platform for Action," written and compiled by Women's Environment and Development Organization, (WEDO), 1995, p. 1. Available from WEDO, 845 Third Avenue, 15th Floor, New York, N.Y. 10022, or e-mail: wedo@igc.apc.org

66. See the *Platform for Action and the Beijing Declaration*, adopted by the Fourth World Conference on Women, Beijing, China, September 4–15 , 1995 (New York: Department of Public Information, United Nations, 1996), especially the section "Women and Health," pp. 56–72.

67. Ibid., see especially "Women and Poverty," pp. 37–46.

68. Quoted in *The Advancement of Women*, p. 5.

69. *From Nairobi to Beijing*, p. 251.

70. Quoted in Sarah Lyall, "Hillary Clinton Sees Hope in Ulster, Too," *New York Times*, November 1, 1997, p. A6.

71. Statement by Gertrude Mongella to the Opening of the 39th

Session of the Commission on the Status of Women, March 15, 1995, New York, p. 12. Available from the United Nations.

72. See *The Progress of Nations* pamphlet, 1995, UNICEF House, 3 United Nations Plaza, New York, N.Y. 10017; and *Weaving a Better Future*, pamphlet prepared for the Women's Environment and Development Organization (WEDO), January 1996.

73. Virginia Vargas, "International Feminist Networking and Solidarity: Toward the VII Latin American and Caribbean Feminist Gathering, Chile 1996," in *Women Living Under Muslim Laws,* Occasional Paper No. 9 (August 1996), pp. 10, 12.

74. *Platform for Action,* pp. 2, 3.

75. Ibid, see "Violence against Women," pp. 73–81.

76. Ibid., see especially, "Human Rights of Women," pp. 121–132.

77. "The Voices of Youth For Beijing Regional Youth Consultations for the Fourth World Conference on Women," Background Paper, March 15, 1995, prepared by the Department for Policy Coordination and Sustainable Development, United Nations.

78. *From Nairobi to Beijing*, p. xi.

79. The World Conference on Human Rights was held in 1993 in Vienna, Austria; the International Conference on Population and Development was convened in 1994 in Cairo, Egypt.

80. *From Nairobi to Beijing*, pp. 125–127.

81. Alice Walker and Pratibha Parmar, *Warrior Marks* (New York: Harcourt Brace, 1993); Linda Burstyn, "Female Circumcision Comes to America", *Atlantic Monthly,* vol. 276, no. 4 (October 1995): 28–35; and Celia Dugger, "Woman's Plea for Asylum Puts Tribal Ritual on Trial," *New York Times,* April 15, 1996, p. A1. For a critique of FGM discussions as part of the 'third-worlding' of African women, see: Claire Robertson, "Grassroots in Kenya: Women, Genital Mutilation, and Collective Action, 1920–1990," *Signs,* vol. 21, no. 3 (spring 1996): 615–642.

82. Asia Watch Women's Rights Project, *A Modern Form of Slavery* (New York: Human Rights Watch, 1993), especially chaps. 4 and 5.

83. Seth Faison, "Women's Meeting Agrees on Right to Say No to Sex," *New York Times,* September 11, 1995, p. A1.

84. *Platform for Action,* see "Women and Health," especially pp. 58–62.

85. Rosalind Pollack Petchesky, "Sexual Rights: Inventing a Concept, Mapping an International Practice," talk delivered at the Conference on Reconceiving Sexuality, Rio de Janeiro, April 14, 1996, p. 2. See also her "Spiralling Discourses of Reproductive and Sexual Rights: A Post-Beijing Assessment of International Feminist Politics," in C. Cohen, K. Jones and J. Tronto, eds., *Women Transforming Politics* (New York: NYU Press, 1997); "Reproductive and Sexual Rights in International Perspective: A Post-Beijing Assessment," paper presented at Rutgers University, Center for the Critical Analysis of Contemporary Culture, October 17, 1995; and "From Population Control to Reproductive Rights: Feminist Fault Lines," *Reproductive Health Matters,* no. 6 (November 1995): 152–61.

86. Arjun Appadurai, *Modernity at Large* (Minneapolis: University of Minnesota Press, 1996), p. 165.

87. Merchant, *Earthcare,* pp. 221, 146.

88. Paid advertisement in the *New York Times,* April 12, 1996, p. A25, sponsored by over a thousand Japanese women.

89. Barbara Crossette, "Muslim Women's Movement Is Gaining Strength," *New York Times,* May 12, 1996, p. A3. See also Margot Badran, *Feminists, Islam, and Nation* (Princeton: Princeton University Press, 1995); and Valentine Moghadam, ed., *Gender and National Identity* (London: Zed Books, 1994).

90. Maria Riley, *Women Connecting, Beyond Beijing* (Washington, D.C.: Center of Concern, 1996), pp. 44, 53.

91. This issue is discussed in the document *Information and Communications in the Beijing Platform for Action,* March 1996, compiled by the International Women's Tribune Centre (IWTC), 777 U.N. Plaza, New York, N.Y. 10017, e-mail: wsource@igc.apc.org

92. For a series of interesting articles about digital bodies and feminism, as well as a feminist yellow pages of cyberspace, see "Sexuality

and Cyberspace," *Women and Performance: A Journal of Feminist Theory*, vol. 9:1, no. 17 (1996).

93. The NOW internet site address is http://www.now.org/ The campaign site is webperson@now.org

94. Posted May 23, 1997 at batshalo@netvision.net.il; one can also contact Bat Shalom of the Jerusalem Link, P.O. Box 8083, Jerusalem 91080, Israel.

95. http://www.womenspace.com/

96. http://www.igc.apc.org/vsister/vsister.html

97. Amelia DeLoach, "Grrrls Exude Attitude," *CMC Magazine (Computer Mediated Communication)*, March 1, 1996, deloaa@rpi.edu or http://www.geekgirl.com.au/geekgirl/index.html

98. http://www.geekgirl.com.au/geekgirl/index.html

99. http://www.filament.illumin.co.uk/ica/Bookshop/video/writerstalk/bodyasmetaph.html

100. From e-mail correspondence, July 11, 1997. E-mail address: uleshedhalle@access.chmanderfu@worldcom.ch internet site: http://www.access.ch/justwatch

101. http://www.feminist.org/other/beijing2.html allows you to visit a huge web of information flowing from these feminist locations.

102. http://wwrl.inre.asu.edu/toc.html

103. These sites are available at http://www.feminist.org/other/beijing2.html

104. http://www.geocities.com/Athens/2533/russfem.html

index

about the author

A noted feminist writer, Zillah Eisenstein is Professor of Politics at Ithaca College. She is the author of *The Female Body and the Law,* which won the Victoria Schuck Book Prize for the best book on women and politics, and, more recently, *The Color of Gender: Reimaging Democracy* and *Hatreds: Racialized and Sexualized Conflicts in the 21st Century.*